The
Leader's
Palette

Seven Primary Colors

RALPH E. ENLOW JR.

WestBow
PRESS
A DIVISION OF THOMAS NELSON

WestBow Press books may be ordered through booksellers or by contacting:

WestBow Press
A Division of Thomas Nelson
1663 Liberty Drive
Bloomington, IN 47403
www.westbowpress.com
1-(866) 928-1240

ISBN: 978-1-4497-8392-1 (sc)
ISBN: 978-1-4497-8394-5 (hc)
ISBN: 978-1-4497-8393-8 (e)

Library of Congress Control Number: 2013902077

Printed in the United States of America

WestBow Press rev. date: 2/7/2013

To Robertson …

> who consistently showed me what leadership is and fearlessly thrust me into it.

In memory of Bob …

> who courageously shaped me as a leader and faithfully traveled the road with me.

Praise for The Leader's Palette

I wish I had read this book 40 years ago! Ralph Enlow masterfully pulls together the wisdom of scores of leadership-training specialists, and outlines a powerful presentation of principles for effective leadership. Designed to help the leader develop his potential to the maximum, *The Leader's Palette: Seven Primary Colors,* will build leadership potential in the beginner or veteran. Not only is the treatment well rooted in broad research, it is laced with fun and serious real-life anecdotes to make the complex clear and to lure toward application.

Robertson McQuilkin, President Emeritus, Columbia International University

Ralph Enlow brilliantly integrates his own significant experience with Scripture, research on leadership, and gems from other authors in this challenging, engaging book. I intend to commend it to friends in leadership, executive coaches, and even search committees. If you aspire to be a Christ-centered leader or teach it to others, this is a must read.

Robert C. Andringa, President Emeritus, Council for Christian Colleges & Universities.

Ever since I met Ralph Enlow many years ago, I have become a student of his. Now with *The Leader's Palette*, you too can become a student and learn from a man of invisible humility and rock solid convictions. With uncanny wisdom, Ralph engages the reader to think about leadership in a unique, multi-dimensional way.
Peter W. Teague, President, Lancaster Bible College

What great leadership wisdom from someone who has thirty years of experience in the trenches of leadership. I really appreciate Ralph's refreshing seven colors approach, since so many leaders excel in one or two strengths but don't operate out of a full "palette" of leadership effectiveness. Like the author, I too have observed many a gifted leader who has neglected to master their art. If you lead and have a passion to reach the fullest expression of your leadership art, then by all means devour this great book.
*Hans Finzel, President of HDLeaders and bestselling author of **The Top Ten Mistakes Leaders Make.***

Ralph Enlow does a great job delineating the various dynamics involved in exercising effective leadership. Well-researched, biblically-based and quite practical, *The Leader's Palette: Seven Primary Colors*, helps the reader quickly see which areas of leadership need strengthening in one's area of service and how to improve them.
Bill Jones, President, Columbia International University

Ralph Enlow provides a fresh and creative rubric for understanding biblical leadership. In a highly readable style, Ralph weaves a fabric of keen biblical insights from the threads of both his study and personal modeling of biblical leadership. The result is a "colorful" conceptual framework providing a clear and fresh presentation of biblical leadership as well as a guide for the application of these principles in becoming a more effective leader. A must read for those seriously desiring to model biblical leadership!

Jim Barnes, President Emeritus, Indiana Wesleyan University

Among thousands of books on biblical leadership it often remains unclear how today's Christian can successfully lead without succumbing to practices of the world around us. Ralph Enlow colorfully inspires us to be radically different and authentic with respect to God's incarnational vision for us. More importantly, Enlow's work celebrates the uniqueness and complexities with which we are all innately endowed in order to accomplish our full potential.

Yvonne Thigpen, President, Evangelical Training Association

Seeing connections in disparate dimensions of life, ones that many of us miss. Ralph Enlow has repeatedly demonstrated that gift as we have reflected together about leadership in Christian higher education. He has done it again in *The Leader's Palette: Seven Primary Colors*. After a thoughtful discussion of whether leaders are born or made and a review of core biblical concepts of leadership, the author focuses on seven "primary colors" of leadership, each of which contributes to holistic description of an ideal leader. I plan to have our leaders at Johnson University read this creative work from one who demonstrates these colors in his own leadership in the academy and the church.

Gary E. Weedman, President, Johnson University

The Leader's Palette is creatively conceived and artfully written. Ralph Enlow paints a well-framed picture of biblical leaders as stewards, servants, and shepherds. Readers will find practical advice ('Never discover, discuss, and decide an issue on the same occasion'), astute observations ('Leaders who can't stop themselves are as toxic as leaders who can't steer themselves'), and memorable principles ('Experience is not the best teacher after all. Experience reflected upon is the best teacher'). This book will be helpful to all who desire to expand their leadership skills.

David Faust, President, Cincinnati Christian University

Ralph Enlow has put into words principles that can help us practitioners hone our leadership skills while also providing us with an excellent textbook to use in our classes on Christian leadership. In writing this book, Ralph has drawn on both his experience as an administrator used to executive leadership practices and also as an academic leader who has led faculty with legislative skill. He demonstrates not only his comprehensive familiarity with leadership theory and literature but also his understanding of what works in leading people—and what does not. I particularly appreciate how Ralph has woven scripture into this masterpiece portrait he has painted with his leadership palette.

Junias V. Venugopal, Provost and Dean of Education, Moody Bible Institute

The Leader's Palette is a unique and compelling approach to a biblical understanding of leadership. Examining leadership through the metaphor of the visual artist, Ralph Enlow challenges influencers to utilize the full spectrum of the leadership "colors" available to them. While making no claim to be the last work in a biblical understanding of leadership, Enlow's overall approach provides keen insights for any leader seeking to grow into the full potential of their God-given leadership gifts. *The Leader's Palette* is highly readable and practical look inside the secret of Ralph's remarkably effective leadership in the diverse worlds of higher education, non-profits, and ministry. I highly recommend it!

Gary D. Stratton, Bethel University
Senior Editor, TwoHandedWarriors.com: Reimagining Faith and Culture One Story at a Time

Table of Contents

List Of Figures

Acknowledgements

I want to acknowledge with sincere gratitude the many people who have contributed to the writing of this volume.

My Father, Ralph Enlow, Sr., passed away before the book was completed. Nevertheless, his steadfast example, lavish encouragement, faithful prayers, and critical review of the text leave an invisible watermark on every page. My mother, Peggy Enlow, languishes under the scourge of Alzheimer's disease, but her imprint upon me as a leader and a person endures.

My wife of 35 years, Valerie, has been a devoted partner, courageous mirror, and unswerving anchor through every step of my leadership journey.

My best friend and best boss ever, Robert Kallgren, succumbed to cancer before the book was completed. For most of the way, he read drafts and prodded me along with his contagious laughter and unflagging friendship.

My long term life and leadership model and sponsor-mentor, Robertson McQuilkin, has put up with my failings and foibles and interceded for me throughout my career up to this very day.

My colleagues on the Association for Biblical Higher Education board and staff have affirmed my ambition to write about leadership and made generous accommodation in order to make it possible.

David Enlow, Ken and Susan Enlow, Kevin and Lainie McWilliams, Robert Ferris, Diana Knutsen, and David Medders read manuscript drafts and provided helpful feedback, wise counsel, and relentless encouragement.

There is no one like my Heavenly Father— infinitely great and infinitely good, to my everlasting astonishment, ever willing to forgive and use me. I implore you to worship him and follow his leadership above all.

Introduction

Erik Larson's *Devil in the White City*[1] is a page-turning historical thriller chronicling the 1892-93 Chicago World's Fair, aka *The World's Columbian Exposition*. Adroitly spinning a chilling, too-strange-to-be-fiction tale, Larson starkly exposes modernism's paradox: the simultaneous revelation of humanity's unbelievable ingenuity and unspeakable depravity. Under architect Daniel Burnham's indefatigable leadership and planning genius, in a dizzying race against time and in the face of relentless condescension and derision from elitist New York and Paris (which unfurled the Eiffel Tower at the previous decade's world fair—an achievement of scale and grandeur believed to be unrepeatable), America's Second City designed and delivered a world's fair venue of astonishing technological brilliance and heart-stopping beauty.

One of Burnham's early leadership coups was to persuade landscape architect Frederick Law Olmstead to accept the enterprise's landscape design commission. Burnham certainly knew how to shoot for the moon. Olmstead was a living legend. Today regarded as the father of landscape architecture, Olmstead had previously masterminded the original design of such landscape masterpieces as New York City's Central Park and Brooklyn's Prospect Park, Boston's Emerald Necklace, and the campuses of Stanford

University and the University of Chicago, to name a few. And did Olmstead ever deliver! He transformed a barren, sandy, 630-acre swamp on Lake Michigan's shore into a memorable and serene series of canals converging in a luminous lagoon around which were configured the *White City's* stunning American Renaissance, neo-classical exposition venues. Olmstead's art inspired Katharine Lee Bates to pen the famous line, "thine alabaster cities gleam undimmed by human tears" in her American heirloom anthem, *America the Beautiful.* In 1893, Burnham aptly characterized his friend Olmstead's genius, as follows: "An artist, he paints with lakes and wooded slopes; with lawns and banks and forest covered hills; with mountain sides and ocean views."

So what does a book about leadership have to do with painting landscapes? Plenty. I think leadership is a lot like painting. It involves certain core elements and requires technical mastery. But these alone do not constitute art. In the hands of a gifted painter, the potential of these elements to express variation and beauty is as vast as God's imagination.

No one who has thought or read much about leadership is oblivious to the debate as to whether leadership is an art or a science, whether leaders are *born* or *made*. On the one hand, I suppose there would be few books on leadership if it were concluded that leaders are *born* and that's all there is to it. The presumably un-endowed might write and read on the subject with admiration, even envy, but without realistic aspiration of ascending in leadership or gaining any measure of proficiency in it. On the other hand, evidence abounds that not everyone is equally capable of leading well. Is this simply because they have not acquired certain techniques which they could, with determination, master and exercise with proficiency equal to the greatest of leaders? It is hard to take that view seriously.

I ask again, are leaders *born* or *made*? I believe the answer is YES. The Bible makes it clear that human beings are endowed with both natural and spiritual gifts and that the distribution of these gifts differs in *kind* and *degree* and, perhaps, *configuration* as well. I Corinthians 12:4 informs us that, "There are different kinds of gifts." Romans 12:6 similarly asserts, "We have different gifts according to the grace given to each of us." In other words, you have been given some gifts I don't have and I have been given some gifts you don't have. Previously, moreover, in verse 3, Paul speaks of gifting as according to, "the measure of faith," suggesting that gifting occurs not only in a variety of abilities but also in a range of capacities. Paul suggests—and I think the entire context of Romans 12 bears this out—that we inflict harm upon ourselves and havoc upon God's people when we overestimate the degree of our giftedness. He warns, "Do not think of yourself more highly than you ought, but rather think of yourself with sober judgment, in accordance with the measure of faith God has distributed to each of you" (Rom. 12:3b).

A superficial reading of these and other Scripture passages might lead you to conclude that leaders are simply *born* and not *made* and that, therefore, efforts to acquire leadership knowledge and skill are foolish and futile. And you would be wrong.

Consider piano playing. Can anyone learn to play the piano? I think the answer is, yes. Given enough time, dedication, exposure to the most effective theories and techniques, and practice—lots of practice—pretty much anyone can learn to play the piano. So there is no such thing as musical gifting, right? Wrong! How do musically gifted people differ from those without such a gift (differences in *kind*)? How easy is it to distinguish between people who have a high degree of musical gifting and those who have much more modest endowments (differences in *degree*)? Gifted people evidence greater aptitude, acquire skill at a quicker rate, and ultimately perform with originality, imagination, and artistic effect that no amount of technical proficiency can approximate. It doesn't take a musicologist to distinguish between a technically proficient pianist and a virtuoso.

The same is true for leadership. There are indeed techniques and skills involved. I intend to talk about some of them in this book. Leadership skills can be articulated, examined, and developed to a certain extent. People of relatively low giftedness can and should develop respectable proficiency in various aspects of leadership when circumstances require. On the other hand, leadership excellence is more than the application of rudimentary techniques and skills. In painting, there are primary pigments, but knowing and applying them does not make you a great painter. Pretty much any of us can recognize the difference between painting by numbers and true art. You can learn certain things about pigments and painting techniques, but your capacity to create great art is not a matter of primary elements and rudimentary technique. On the other hand, what a pathetic waste when someone with staggering artistic ability omits some of the basic ingredients or declines to master basic tools and techniques.

So, that settles it, leaders are *born*, right? As colorful ESPN football analyst Lee Corso would say, "Not so fast, my friend." It is true that there is such a thing as a gift of leadership and that people with leadership gifts are distinguishable from people who lack the gift. On the other hand, just as in piano playing, leadership involves proficiency in a complex array of dispositions, skills, and techniques. It is precisely because leadership is a gift that those who have been so gifted must dedicate themselves to growing their *proficiency* in exercising this gift and realizing the full *capacity* with which they have been endowed. It is worse than tragic, it is dangerous when those who have leadership gifts rely on gifting alone, failing to appropriate the Spirit's grace and power and to invest the time and effort necessary to unwrap the gift's full potential by study and reflective practice. People can learn to lead. Gifted people, most of all, need to learn how to exercise their gifts. There are insights and skills to be gained by the diligent. Are you called upon to lead but unsure of your gifting? You can better assess and develop your gifting by studying the principles in this book. Are you gifted to lead? You can take your leadership to new levels as you expand your portfolio of proficiencies.

I have a friend who has a prodigious musical gift. He can listen to a classical concerto or Broadway show tune and play it from memory. His musical styling bears the unmistakable marks of artistry. I have heard him enthrall audiences of strangers with an impromptu concert in a St. Moritz hotel ballroom. He can accommodate pretty much any audience request. But he can barely read music. He struggles to play accurately the simple score of a church hymnal. He plays in only one key. He can't accompany a soloist or play in a band. Is he gifted? By all means! Apparently, his gifting is similar to what we know about Mozart. But, has he, like Mozart, *developed* the skills necessary to fully exercise his gift, has he reached his full *capacity* as a musician? Not at all. You see, we will never know the extent of my friend's musical gift nor enjoy the full splendor of his art because he has not, through disciplined study and diligent practice, acquired the technical knowledge, mastered the skills, and developed the proficiencies associated with musical greatness.

I think a lot of leaders are like my piano player friend. They may be gifted, but they have neglected to master their art. They are proficient in only one or two leadership "keys"—or *colors*, to use the metaphor I have chosen for this book. They refuse to listen and learn. In short, they rely on their giftedness which, in some cases is quite prodigious, but fail to acquire and hone to their fullest capacity the full spectrum of dispositions and skills available to them as leaders. Many such leaders I recognize to be people of deep piety and sincere commitment to serve the Lord. The grace of God is clearly evident in their lives and through their leadership. Nevertheless, their leadership does not result in the fullness of beauty and *shalom* God had in mind when he gifted and called them to lead. In some cases, they wreak organizational havoc and inflict personal injury upon those for whom they have been given charge. In other cases, they and their followers simply writhe in drudgery, dissipation or despair.

Giftedness is accompanied by responsibility and the greater the gift, the greater the responsibility. If there is any possibility that you may have the gift of leadership, you have an obligation to make it your lifelong ambition to master as fully as possible the entire array of dispositions and skills necessary for the godly, effective exercise of your gift. Will you be a great leader? Only God knows the range of your capabilities and the extent of the capacities he has implanted in you. He is eager to reveal and release them as you commit yourself to developing your fullest potential in the unfolding of his providence. I pray this book will help you along that path.

For more than thirty years, I have been a thoughtful observer of leaders good and bad. I have studied, reflected, and taught about leadership informed by extensive biblical, professional, and social science reading and research. I have exercised my leadership calling—sometimes disgracefully and sometimes, by the grace of God, with fruitfulness and fulfillment far beyond my deserving—in local church, higher education, and mission agency contexts. Over time, I have concluded that leadership involves seven primary elements, or *colors*, as I refer to them in this book. I am convinced that highly gifted leaders should devote themselves to understanding, mastering, and working in harmony with the properties of each of these elements—not merely one or two—if they are to reach the fullest expression of their art and, thus, achieve the blessing for which they have been gifted to lead.

Before I get to the primary *colors*, I should let you know what I mean by leadership. I agree with many others who have thought and written on the subject that leadership is not primarily about *position*. You may be in a position of leadership and not be leading; you can lead without being in a leadership position. John Maxwell states it succinctly: "The proof of leadership is found in the followers." ² Take heed: If no one is following, you need to give serious thought as to whether—or at least how—you are leading.

So if leadership is not primarily about position, what is it about? In essence, leadership is *influence*. I think Ted Engstrom rendered it about as accurately and succinctly as anyone: "A leader is a person people will follow in a given situation."³ It's really no more complicated than that. A leader is simply someone who influences people such that they are willing to follow in terms of a given manner and direction. For the Christ-follower, leadership of course means godly, biblical, Spirit-empowered influence—but its essence still involves influence more than position. Here's how I sum it up. If you have an aversion to alliteration (oops, sorry!) hold your nose: **A leader is a person who serves as a catalyst for collective clarity, community, change or convergence toward accomplishment of consequential ends.** Note that this definition suggests both how a leader *acts* and what a leader *accomplishes*.

The leader *acts* as a *catalyst*. I much prefer the term *catalyst* to something like *commander*. This preference reflects my informed persuasion regarding biblical teaching, insights from professional literature, and social science research findings. It is not always necessary—though sometimes it may be required—for leaders to issue orders. Mostly, however, leaders help to bring about certain effects by whatever means and style may be appropriate (more about that in chapter 7). The leader does this less by issuing commands that merely result in behavioral compliance than by working as a *catalyst* to elicit followership that results in deeper levels of mutual commitment.

Effective leaders accomplish results in several dimensions. They help to influence *clarity* in terms of an organization's context and circumstances as well as the ends for which it exists and appropriate ways and means of pursuing those ends. They also influence *community*—a sense of belonging, identity, solidarity, mutuality among an organization's members and even its external stakeholders. Leaders help people navigate *change* where required by circumstances and influence *convergence* of effort and resources toward the ends that matter for time and eternity.

How do leaders generate influence? I believe they do so by judiciously selecting, blending, and applying one or more of seven primary elements. I like to think of them as the leader's palette. The more leaders master and incorporate each primary pigment and the more gracefully and imaginatively they blend these seven *colors*, the more satisfying and even astonishing may be the effects of their leadership. So what are these primary areas of leadership influence, these primary *colors*? Leaders garner influence and gain followers by making effective use of as many of the following elements as possible:

- Primary Color #1: *Incarnational* Leadership. Leaders lead much more by their character and dispositions than their craft and directives.
- Primary Color #2: *Relational* Leadership. Leaders lead through authentic relationships much more than through issuing directives and implementing organizational schemes.
- Primary Color #3: *Developmental* Leadership. Leaders lead by identifying, developing, and releasing the giftedness of those for whom they have leadership responsibility much more than through the exercise of their own capacities, no matter how prodigious.
- Primary Color #4: *Directional* Leadership. Leaders lead by helping stakeholders to clarify and coalesce around a coherent mission and compelling vision.
- Primary Color #5: *Ecological* Leadership. Leaders lead by exercising environmental sensitivity and skill: nurturing a community identity, engendering and espousing shared values, and cultivating a wholesome organizational climate.
- Primary Color #6: *Situational* Leadership. Leaders lead by seeking optimal fit or adaptation to variable and changing situational factors.
- Primary Color #7: *Doxological* Leadership. Leaders lead by fostering people's movement toward God and with God, exercising their power in godly ways and for godly ends.

The remainder of this book will expose you to these seven primary *colors* one by one. Entire books could be—well, actually, have been—written about each element. My purpose here is to help you see the entire palette before you start experimenting with individual pigments and the infinite combinations that can make your leadership art truly original and inspiring. As you read about and ponder each *color*, you might assess the extent of your awareness and proficiency with regard to that particular element. Where you have inadequately considered or ineptly applied one or more *colors* in your previous or present leadership responsibilities, note that I have referenced additional resources that may be helpful as you seek to develop further your understanding, appreciation, and dexterity in the use of those elements.

I begin, however, with a more thorough look at the paradoxical way the Bible talks about leadership. Take a look at chapter one.

Chapter One

Leadership in Biblical Terms

Leadership is an explosive commodity. I believe it is universally axiomatic that a thing's potential for evil is directly proportional to its potential for good. Leadership has enormous potential for good but, alas, colossal potential for harm. Perhaps that explains the Bible's apparent ambivalence about leadership. On the one hand, you can scarcely turn to a book of the Bible and fail to encounter a significant leader through whom God has chosen to work. The biblical narrative has a disproportional focus upon leaders. I think it fair to say that, when God wants something done, he raises up a leader.

Consider the times of the judges. The entire book of Judges revolves around ten cycles that read like an ancient version of the movie *Ground Hog Day*. Israel, peaceful and prosperous, becomes apathetic, forsakes God, devolves into moral degeneracy and social barbarism, gets marauded, invaded, and ravaged by pagan adversaries, wallows in national distress. Time after time God, "… raised up judges [the Hebrew word *sophet* refers generically to a person who governs] who saved them out of the hands of these raiders ..." (Judges 2:16). What means does God choose to restore justice, rescue from oppression, and renew *shalom* among his wayward covenant people? Leaders!

You must not, however, let it escape your notice that the Bible goes out of its way to distinguish the sort of leaders God has in mind for his people from conventional pagan terms and notions. This distinction seems to me to be at the root of God's disgust with Israel's insistence upon having a king. Clearly, God intended for Israel to be led. Beginning with Moses, continuing with Joshua and a 300-year succession of judges up to the time of Samuel, the Lord designates and uses leaders to govern his people. Judges dispensed justice, arbitrated disputes, ensured citizen welfare and security, led the community in spiritual inquiry and renewal of worship, sought and followed Divine direction toward Israel's promised destiny. In so doing, they wielded no intrinsic authority. Rather, judges mediated the rule of Jehovah himself, Israel's covenant King (see I Sam. 8:7; Isa. 33:22). But that wasn't good enough for Israel. Instead of embracing and exulting in their distinctiveness from other nations, incorrigible Israel insisted, "... now appoint a king to lead us, *such as all the other nations have*" (I Sam. 8:5) [emphasis added].

What was so repugnant about the notion of a king *such as all the other nations have*? First, Scripture informs us that insistence on keeping up with the pagans was a rejection of the rule of God. The LORD says to Samuel, "... it is not you they have rejected, but they have rejected me as their king" (I Sam. 8:7). Second, Scripture makes it clear from cover to cover that God intends for leadership exercised in his name to be radically different from that which is normative throughout human civilization. What typifies the "kings" of all the other nations? Self-authenticating, self-perpetuating, self-aggrandizing exploitation. Worldly leaders express, sometimes subtly, sometimes shamelessly, the sentiments of Nebuchanezzar: "Is this not the great Babylon I have built as the royal residence, by my mighty power and for the glory of my majesty?" (Dan. 4:30). Ironically, Nebuchadnezzar's own testimony, recorded in Scripture, tells us, "... the words were on his lips ..." (Dan. 4:31) when he received his comeuppance from the King of Heaven.

Three Biblical Leadership Designations

The God-breathed text of Scripture typically declines to employ terminology ordinarily associated with secular political and military leaders with regard to leaders of God's people. From Oswald Sanders' classic, *Spiritual Leadership,*[4] I first learned that common Hebrew leadership designations like *nagid* (man at the top) and *ro'osh* (head) and Greek terms like *arche* (literally the one "above") and *hodegos* (guide, leader of the way) are rarely used to describe leaders among God's people. Instead, the most common terms of scriptural- and self-designation employed concerning godly leaders are these: **servant** (Hebrew: *ebed*; Greek: *doulos*, *huperetes*, *oikonomos*) and **shepherd** (Hebrew: *ra'ah*; Greek: *poimein*, *poimaino*). Further analysis of the usage of these terms suggests that a biblical conception of leadership revolves around three primary metaphors: **steward, servant, shepherd.**[5] Let's take a closer look at each of these metaphors.

Steward. Biblical usage of terms commonly translated **servant** seems to fall into two complementary but distinctive classifications. The first usage category typically is rendered as the servant **of the LORD**. Scripture employs this designation, "the servant of the LORD" as the most common way of referring to God's covenant leaders from Abraham to Isaiah. It serves as a sort of Scriptural epitaph for Moses (Deut. 34:5), Joshua (Josh. 24:29), David (1 Kings 8:25; 1 Chron. 17:24), and Elijah (2 Kings 10:10). Even our Lord Jesus Christ is characterized as a servant of this order by the Prophets and Gospel narrators! The Apostle Paul embraced the metaphor as well, preferring to call himself "the bondslave of Christ" (employing the even more menial terms of *huperetos* – galley slave, and *diakonos* – table server).

Used in this way, the word **servant** might better be understood as agent, manager, emissary, or **steward** (the term I have chosen to use). The sacred obligation of a steward is to exercise oversight of another's beloved or belongings, do the other's bidding, act on the other's behalf, and accrue to the other's benefit. To be a leader is first, then, to be a servant *of* the LORD.

Stewards' significance is found not in terms of the domain *over which* they are sovereign but the Sovereign *under whom* they serve. Moreover, a steward is not so much a person *in* authority as a person *under* authority. Although it entails delegated authority—authority which is meant to be recognized and ratified by God's people (see, for example, Exodus 5:29-31)—the primary implication of stewardship is accountability. Stewards must account for how fittingly they represent their master's regime and how faithfully they conduct their master's business. Stewards do not pursue their personal agenda, assert personal authority, seek personal acclaim, and accumulate personal assets. Their honor derives from their master's status and their success is defined by their master's satisfaction.

Servant. Analysis of biblical references to God's leaders as **servants** reveals a second cluster of meaning. Scripture strongly repudiates an aristocratic notion of leadership together with all of its accompanying manifestations and abuses. In his extensive biblical theology of leadership, my former colleague Donald Howell writes,

Formal leadership in the secular or religious world is always a moral test. To be placed in a position of influence over others often means the enjoyment of higher monetary remuneration, social prestige, the admiration of one's peers, and the internal satisfaction of having achieved vocational success. The rewards of prominence are why leadership positions are eagerly pursued and jealously guarded. However, elevation brings with it heightened opportunities for the vices of greed, arrogance, and vanity to creep in and overtake one's soul.[6]

Leadership that befits the character and calling of God steadfastly resists the trappings and temptations associated with elevated status. In fact, the Bible turns the association between leadership and status entirely upside down. Scripture calls leaders to a humble demeanor, a lowly posture toward those over whom the leader has been given charge. Jesus declared war on the religious leadership status quo of his day. He railed against contemptible Pharisaical practices of insistence upon special titles, symbols, and rituals that perpetuate social distance and command subordinates' deference (see Mt. 23).

Considering the subtlety and permeability of sub-biblical leadership values, we should not be surprised to discover that even those disciples in whom Jesus' teaching and training efforts were most extensively invested were deeply infected with perverse notions of what a position of leadership entails. We are told that as Jesus' mission marched toward its presumed culmination, the disciples engaged in an increasingly petty dispute and resorted to craven maneuvering—to the point of James and John attempting to leverage their mother's influence—relative to their personal status in the much-anticipated new regime. Jesus scolded them: "You know that those who are regarded as rulers of the Gentiles lord it over them, and their high officials exercise authority over them. *Not so with you.* Instead, whoever wants to become great among you must be your servant, and whoever wants to be first must be slave of all" (Mk. 10:42-44) [emphasis added]. Jesus' most extensive exposition on this subject, recorded most fully in Matthew 18, instructs us that greatness in his realm would find expression in:

- childlike humility instead of entitlement;
- preoccupation with the weak and vulnerable instead of pandering for patronage;
- joyful affirmation instead of envy;
- moral vigilance instead of moral indulgence;
- priorities aligned with God's redemptive heart instead of public popularity;
- redemptive pursuit of reconciliation with offenders instead of condemnation and separation; and
- profound extravagance toward others born of a profound sense of indebtedness to God for his extravagance toward us instead of petty retribution.

Though the disciples' overt campaigning may have subsided following Jesus' discourse on servant leadership, it persisted in perhaps more subtle and insidious ways. Sequestered with his future kingdom leadership core to celebrate the Passover meal on the night before his betrayal, Jesus observed that no one took upon himself the menial hospitality ritual of foot washing. Given the weight of the occasion and the urgency of the final revelations to be made that night, you or I might have been inclined to minimize and rationalize this relatively insignificant omission. Jesus took a different view. This was no mere social slight. It exposed the root of an attitude that, if not confronted, would corrupt the entire Gospel enterprise. Indeed, it has corrupted a good deal of what passes for Christianity right up to the present. John tells us (Jn. 13:3-4) that, with full knowledge of his regal identity and destiny, Jesus ceremoniously arose from the table, girded himself with a towel, filled a water basin, and performed the stinky service. This provoked the predictable reaction of horror, shame, and insensibility—and afforded the teachable moment Jesus sought. He declared, "Now that I, your Lord and Teacher, have washed your feet, you also should wash one another's feet" (Jn. 13:14).

In writing to the Philippians, among whom were apparently many vestiges of pagan relational and leadership patterns, the Apostle Paul reveals that Jesus' countercultural, upside down leadership values were communicated not merely by exhortation but most of all by example. In Philippians 2:1-11, Paul reveals that the Second Person of the Trinity, co-equal and co-eternal with the Father and Spirit, took up the demeanor of a bond-servant, voluntarily waived his right to the free exercise of his divine prerogatives, and humbly submitted himself to the powerlessness of a humiliating criminal execution. What did becoming a servant entail for Jesus? It meant relinquishing his rights, rank, and reputation. Most leaders—I fear even too many Christian leaders—act as if those are precisely the things to which a leader is entitled. They are considered the rewards of "service." There are rewards for service. But Scripture instructs us that God's kingdom leaders should reckon that they come in proportion to the forfeit of rights, rank, and reputation. Note that instead of forfeiting his reward, Jesus' submission to suffering was the path to his inheritance of it.

Shepherd. A third pervasive Scriptural metaphor for leaders is **shepherd**. Shepherds devote themselves to the duty of providing for the welfare of their flocks by offering nourishment, guidance, and protection. Leaders who shepherd well are emulating the greatest Shepherd of all—the Lord himself. Jacob—now and ever after known as Israel—in offering a patriarchal blessing to Joseph from his deathbed, acknowledges, "... the God who has been my shepherd all my life, to this day" (Gen. 48:15). Psalm 23 stands as the most endearing and memorable portrayal of this metaphor with reference to God. In this brief and oft-memorized poem, David echoes his ancestor Jacob in affirming that Jahweh leads him as the perfect Shepherd. The relentless, merciful love of the Shepherd ensures that his charges lack nothing that is required for their flourishing. He feeds and shelters, renews and guides, accompanies and protects, defends and regales, welcomes and secures. Later, Isaiah characterizes David's antecedent and descendant, Jesus Christ, as One who, "tends his flock, like a shepherd" (Isa. 40:11).

Leaders of God's people are also called shepherds. As such, they are expected to emulate the most divine Shepherd. Speaking through the prophets—Jeremiah, Ezekiel, and Zechariah in particular—God rails against the obstinate, abusive, parasitical behavior of Israel's priests. They are guilty of perverting God's truth, indulging in idolatry, engaging in hypocritical moral decadence, failing to protect the weak and vulnerable, and profiting from exploitation. Jesus put his followers on notice early in his ministry that such corruption of the sacred obligations of shepherding among leaders of God's people would not be tolerated. He repeatedly confronted the entitlement culture and all its manifestations among religious leaders of his day, culminating in his virtual impeachment of the rogue Jewish priesthood at the Feast of Dedication (see Jn. 10). He infuriated the Jewish priests and elders by asserting that he was the authentic Good Shepherd and that they had proven themselves to be imposters. In a claim both to his deity and legitimacy as a leader after the pattern of Jacob's and David's and all Israel's divine Shepherd, Jesus proclaims, "I am the good shepherd" (Jn. 10:11, 14,). In so doing, he is of course proclaiming his deity, but also he is declaring in no uncertain terms how a legitimate godly leader behaves.

Peter leads in the extension of this metaphor to church and spiritual leadership of all kinds. Jesus' words of restoration and re-commissioning, "Take care of my sheep" (Jn. 21:16) must have reverberated in Peter's mind in especially powerful ways. Peter, of all Jesus' disciples, might have had cause to claim elevated status. After all, he was the one who first confessed, "You are the Messiah, the Son of the Living God" (Mt. 16:16). It was he who, admittedly humbled by failure, was nevertheless the primary spokesperson on Pentecost and other occasions (Acts 2, 3), the conduit of healing power (Acts 3, 5), the object of an angelic escort out of prison (Acts 4), the pronouncer of Divine judgment upon Ananias and Sapphira (Acts 5), and the recipient of a new revelation about Gentile inclusion (Acts 10). Far from riding these extraordinary privileges into the patriarchal stratosphere, however, the New Testament leaves the impression that Peter's leadership "star" faded behind those of James and Paul. He rejected any claim to infallibility and submitted himself to Paul's public rebuke when, in Antioch, he was intimidated by a Jerusalem "circumcision contingent" into hypocritical adherence to ceremonial scruples (Gal. 2:11-21). Instead of exhibiting a residue of bitterness toward Paul for his rebuke, Peter later described Paul as "our dear brother" and invested his substantial credibility in attesting that the writings of Paul should be regarded as commensurate with "the other Scriptures" (2 Pet. 3:15-16).

A man of great prominence, you might even say spiritual eminence, Peter declines to leverage these credentials in his exercise of leadership. How does he describe himself? To what "authority" does he appeal? He offers the following bona fides: "… I appeal as a fellow elder and a witness of Christ's sufferings who also will share in the glory to be revealed…" (1 Pet. 5:1). He now exhorts church elders scattered throughout the Roman world to, "Be shepherds of God's flock that is under your care …" (1 Pet. 5:2). In the following verses, note the echoes of Old Testament prophecy and Jesus' teaching relative to false and true shepherding:

> Be shepherds of God's flock that is under your care, watching over them—not because you must, but because you are willing, as God wants you to be; not pursuing dishonest gain, but eager to serve; not lording it over those entrusted to you, but being examples to the flock. And when the Chief Shepherd appears, you will receive the crown of glory that will never fade away. In the same way, you who are younger, submit yourselves to your elders. All of you, clothe yourselves with humility toward one another, because, "God opposes the proud but shows favor to the humble." Humble yourselves, therefore, under God's mighty hand, that he may lift you up in due time. Cast all your anxiety on him because he cares for you. Be alert and of sober mind. Your enemy the devil prowls around like a roaring lion looking for someone to devour. Resist him, standing firm in the faith, because you know that the family of believers throughout the world is undergoing the same

kind of sufferings. And the God of all grace, who called you to his eternal glory in Christ, after you have suffered a little while, will himself restore you and make you strong, firm and steadfast. To him be the power for ever and ever. Amen. (1 Peter 5:2-11)

If the leader's palette has seven primary colors, you might say the brush is comprised of three primary fibers. What makes leadership biblical and God-honoring? The difference will not be discerned by what ingredients and techniques are employed. Rather, leadership is distinctively biblical in terms of the *means* by which the basic ingredients and techniques are employed. Biblical leadership is radically different in character from what is practiced and lauded in our world. Nothing could be clearer in Scripture than that God wants leadership in his name and among his people to be practiced according to values that differ greatly from the secular norm.

In summary, Scripture presents three pervasive metaphors by which to pattern our leadership. Godly leaders are like **stewards, servants, shepherds.** These metaphors anchor our leadership by answering three key questions every leader needs to know the answer to:

Steward: *Who Is My Boss?*
Servant: *What Is My Status?*
Shepherd: *What Is My Job?*

With brush firmly in hand, now let's turn to the palette ...

Chapter Two

Primary Color #1:
Incarnational *Leadership*

Perhaps the most indelible *primary color* on the leader's palette is what I (and many others) call *incarnational* leadership. Of all the colors in the palette, this is one of the most consequential—for good or ill. By *incarnational* I simply mean that leadership is much more about *being* than *doing*. Leaders lead through authentic relationships much more than through issuing directives and implementing organizational schemes. This is leadership in terms of *person* not *position* or *process*.

If you accept the notion that *influence* is essential to the definition of leadership, this should be obvious. We influence people far more by who we are than anything we direct them to do. "Do as I say, not as I do" is a formula for leadership disaster. Consequences of corrupt *incarnational* leadership manifest themselves in more than impeded organizational achievement. Serious personal deficiencies in a leader not only cause the leadership process to break down to the detriment of the mission, but also leaders inevitably convey their congenital weaknesses to their followers. Jesus taught that, "The student is not above the teacher, but everyone who is fully trained will be like their teacher" (Lk. 6:40). Leaders cannot escape the fact that they are transmitting their moral and dispositional DNA to successive generations of followers.

We exercise *incarnational* leadership in infinite ways—as numerous and varied as our uniqueness. Paul affirmed the *incarnational* nature of leadership by encouraging the Corinthian and Thessalonian believers to imitate his example as he sought to imitate the Lord (see I Cor. 4:16, 11:1; I Thess. 1:6, 3:7, 3:9). The writer to the Hebrews exhorts his readers to, "Remember your leaders, who spoke the word of God to you. Consider the outcome of their way of life and imitate their faith" (Heb. 13:7). Whatever else *incarnational* leadership means for a follower of Christ, it can mean nothing less than seeking to imitate the Lord in every aspect of life. The totality of our example equals the totality of our *incarnational* leadership.

We might say that we lead, above all, by example, and leave it at that. Nevertheless, I believe it is worthwhile to examine several key aspects of a leader's *being* that, from my personal reading, experiences, and reflection on the subject, are among the most highly consequential in a leadership dynamic. Leaders increase their personal potency when they diligently attend to developing and maintaining their *being* in at least the following key ways: authenticity, discipline, centeredness, accessibility, growth, and grace. Let's take a closer look at each of these ingredients of *incarnational* leadership.

<u>Authenticity</u>. James Kouzes and Barry Posner have led one of the most extensive contemporary global research efforts concerning executive level leadership for more than two decades. Now in

its fourth edition after over 20 years in print, research efforts behind Kouzes and Posner's book, *The Leadership Challenge*[7] have repeatedly validated a five-fold conceptual framework they call, "The Five Practices of Exemplary Leadership." According to Kouzes and Posner, leaders:

- Model the Way
- Inspire a Shared Vision
- Challenge the Process
- Enable Others to Act
- Encourage the Heart

The primary research behind Kouzes and Posner's conceptual framework involves asking leaders at all levels to describe their most successful and satisfying leadership experiences. But Kouzes and Posner have gone further. They reason that if a leader is a person others willingly follow, it would be highly instructive to probe more specifically what it is that makes a leader someone people want to follow. Their findings are contained in a subsequent work, *Credibility: How Leaders Gain and Lose It, Why People Demand It.*[8] Kouzes and Posner asked followers, "What do you look for and admire in a leader, someone whose direction you would *willingly* follow?"[9] They discovered that responses clustered around four attributes they sum up as "credibility." A leader that people are eager to follow looks like this:

- Honest (DWYSYWD – *do what you say you will do*)
- Forward Looking (I'll have more to say about this in chapter five)
- Inspiring (Again, I'll have more to say about this in chapter five)

- Competent (In other words, knowledgeable about the enterprise they lead)

Did you notice which leadership quality shows up when you look at leadership from the vantage point of *both* leaders and followers? That's right—the consistent, believable nature of the leader's personal character. Leadership begins with authenticity and integrity.

I once observed Erwin McManus illustrating integrity by tossing a banana into the audience. He asks the person who catches it, "What is that in your hands?" When the predictable reply comes, "It's a banana," McManus objects, "How do you know? All I see is a banana peel. How do you know it's a banana?" McManus posits that we can have confidence that what is inside a banana peel is indeed a banana because everything God makes has integrity. What is on the inside is invariably consistent with what is presented on the outside. We never peel a banana and find an apple or an apricot. Integrity simply means that what is on the inside is consistent with what is on the outside. Just as in nature, so also in the leader-follower dynamic of influence, we have every right to be astonished and disappointed when inconsistency is discovered between internal and external reality.

Without pressing the metaphor too far, let me suggest that we may be disappointed when we peel a banana and discover a defect. But we are not surprised at imperfection, nor do we regard the banana to be worthless. Defects are common, perhaps even inevitable in a broken world. No leader is without defect. In fact, it is pretension to the contrary that constitutes a lack of authenticity. Leaders are admired and followed not only because they are virtuous but also because they are genuine. And genuineness requires acknowledgement of flaws and failures. Gordon McDonald writes concerning the nature of genuineness:

> My own redemption from a secret-driven life began when I went away to boarding school and came under the influence of worthy men and women who modeled healthy relationships and great faith. The redemption continued in my marriage to a remarkable woman, Gail, with whom I have now shared almost 49 years of life. From her I learned that no amount of appearance-management would ever establish me as truly "fine." The fact is that I am "unfine" by nature. True "fineness" comes slowly and reaches its crescendo at a time known only to God.[10]

There is a difference, however, between imperfection and a fundamental lack of integrity. Substantial inconsistency between internal and external reality is as incongruous in leadership as it is in nature. Deceit, duplicity, and hypocrisy subvert and corrupt leadership. Cancerous cells in a leader metastasize, pervading and perverting the people and organizations over which cynical or hypocritical leaders preside.

Discipline. When you think of a disciplined person, what comes to your mind? Perhaps your experience differs from mine, but my earliest leadership icons inclined me to picture a disciplined person as a *driven* person. Leaders I was taught to admire were men and women of compulsive effort, herculean accomplishment, unrelenting endeavor, and perennial over-extension. While such people seemed to be esteemed by all, they also left the impression that leadership success and personal flameout were synonymous. I have since learned that driven-ness more frequently belies a serious lack of discipline.

I define discipline as the serene center of equilibrium between two poles: impulsiveness on one extreme and compulsiveness on the other (see figure 2.1). An impulsive person follows every whim to the neglect of an anchoring purpose and persevering productivity. A compulsive person cannot resist the urge to speak, act, emote, pursue, achieve—even when it is detrimental to self and counterproductive to others. Leaders who can't stop themselves are as toxic as leaders who can't steer themselves. Lack of discipline ultimately issues in erratic behavior and emotional instability. These tendencies adversely affect both people's inclination and ability to follow consistently. Discipline is nothing less than the outworking of stewardship in every aspect of life. Keeping to the essentials, however, I would like to suggest that discipline involves at least the following key dimensions: restraint and rhythm, and resources.

Self-Control Continuum

Figure 2.1

Discipline certainly means restraint. Perhaps this is the essence of what the Bible means when it speaks of "self-control." Proverbs warns, "Like a city whose walls are broken through is a person who lacks self-control" (Prov. 25:28). Self-control is an aspect of the fruit of the Spirit (Gal. 5:23). Peter instructs us that self-control is an essential building block toward godliness and a fruitful faith (I Pet. 1:5-8). Deficits in self-control often manifest themselves not only in poor time management but also in destructive excesses of temper and tongue. Leaders recognize the critical influence their self-control, or lack thereof, exerts upon their effectiveness in each of these areas. They take inventory of themselves, seek to elevate their practice of these disciplines (or habituated virtues,[11] or habitudes,[12] as others have called them) and invite others to rebuke and correct them when they exhibit weakness, whether subtly or sensationally. Frankly, I was not rebuked often enough for my youthful excesses in temper and tongue. One of my most cherished friendships to this day is with a brother who did not hesitate to give me a stern lecture, rebuking look, or even a good kick under the table when I behaved too boorishly or spoke too testily in a meeting with colleagues.

Discipline also involves rhythm. Although disciplined people can generate a remarkable intensity of effort, they demonstrate that they need not work all the time. There is ebb and flow to their lives. They cultivate and carry out steady rhythms of life, healthy patterns of eating and sleeping, of exertion and diversion. High performance and personal renewal involves energy management more than time management, as Jim Loehr and Tony Schwartz extensively document in their intriguing book, *The Power of Full Engagement.*[13]

Some years ago, I read Paul Johnson's lucid biography of Winston Churchill, regarded by many to be the most significant human figure of the 20th century. To say that Churchill was a prodigious man is the epitome of understatement. He demanded from himself and others a daunting level of intensity. Johnson estimates that the total of his printed words generated over his lifetime approaches 10 million, including his more than 2-million-word account of World War II. While by no means were all of Churchill's personal characteristics and habits of life commendable—far from it—it is noteworthy that Churchill exemplifies a disciplined leader's mastery of rhythm. In summarizing the "factors and virtues that operated in his favor" as a supremely effective leader, Johnson writes, "Churchill's sheer energy and, not least, his ability to switch it off abruptly when not needed, were central keys to his life ...."[14] Churchill devoted himself just as intensively to restorative leisure activities, such as brick-laying and painting, as he did to the exercise of his critical world leadership. I'm told that Rick Warren originated this useful aphorism concerning the discipline of rhythm: *divert daily; withdraw weekly; abandon annually.*

Disciplined leaders practice the principle of Sabbath. Sabbath does not mean cessation of activity. It means deliberate diversion to the most fundamentally restorative of all activities—contemplation and worship of God, not only in solitude but also in the company of God's people. When we fail to observe this principle, we not only dishonor God, we tempt ourselves and others to believe that we ourselves are the fountain of our productivity and success. To the extent leaders manage themselves in the matter of rhythms and rest, they also steward the human and organizational resources entrusted to them. We cultivate in ourselves and model to our followers Sabbath rhythms not because it will help us get our work done better, but because in so doing we are confessing that the work is *for* God and the harvest comes *from* God.

Finally, and perhaps surprisingly to you, discipline is an expression of our disposition toward resources. This is what I mean when I say that discipline is the outworking of stewardship. It includes stewardship of a person's impulses, appetites, capacities, and resources. According to Jesus, this discipline is often, if not always, a barometer of true discipleship (see, for example, Mt. 6:24; Lk. 18:18-30, 19:11-27). It escapes most people's notice, but the first Scriptural mention of Barnabas occurs in connection with his disposition toward resources. Luke tells us that, "Joseph, a Levite from Cyprus, whom the apostles called Barnabas (which means 'son of encouragement') sold a field he owned and brought the money and put it at the apostles' feet" (Acts 4:36-37). Barnabas exhibited many admirable characteristics that contributed to his impact as an early church leader. Arguably the most fundamental, however, was his disposition toward resources. More than in any other way, Barnabas' act of surrendering resources to God demonstrated that he was trustworthy. Leaders exert profound *incarnational* influence when they show that they have settled the issue of ownership and they consistently practice good stewardship of God's resources—human, material, and financial—over which they exercise personal or organizational discretion. Some years ago, a management consultant startled me when he stated that 80% of management comprises allocation of resources. If that estimate conforms to any extent to reality, it means that resource attitudes and dispositions are a central, not marginal, aspect of leadership. There is no room for extravagance and exploitation, greed and gratification, among God's leaders.

By the same token, leaders need to understand the difference between an investment and an expense. Investments pay dividends. Expenses dissipate. The Bible encourages liberal sowing. Faith demands it. Yet, Scripture repeatedly warns against the connection between resources and subversion of a leader's motives. When leaders disproportionately hoard or flaunt resources, treat themselves extravagantly and their colleagues frugally (the more subtle way to do this is through institutional budget allocations rather than personal compensation), or otherwise misappropriate the things over which their station gives them substantial discretion, they betray an ugly and potentially fatal lack of discipline.

Centeredness. Leaders who exert favorable *incarnational* influence are well-anchored in terms of personal mission and motives. They refrain from equating a particular leadership role with their calling. While a given role may be an ideal expression of their calling, indeed a Divine assignment, their mission is of deeper and more enduring nature. In describing what he calls, "The Discipline of Mission," Reggie McNeal writes,

> I have been around countless numbers of spiritual leaders who are dying to hear, "Everyone is looking for you." Their personal sense of worth is determined by being sought after or needed. So they give away their vitality and missional direction to whomever or whatever the need of the hour is or the latest crisis (sometimes a crisis they themselves created!).
>
> Great leaders have not escaped these temptations. They do not lack for opportunities. But they do not chase every one. Nor are they sheltered from people's needs. But they understand that the need is not necessarily the call for them to engage it. They do not lack challenges. But they know that they do not have to fight every fight or take every cause. Great leaders pick the causes, seize the opportunities, and address the needs that fall in line with their mission.[15]

Imagine how Jesus' effectiveness would have been dissipated had he sought directly to confront every injustice, fulfill every demand, indulge every aspiration that crossed his path. At the height of audience demand, he demurred and withdrew when he recognized the clamoring crowd's agenda was inconsistent with his mission. He was often misunderstood because he was so rigorously rooted in a sense of mission. The fact that, as He breathed his last on the cross, he could say with full assurance, "It is finished" testifies that he did so.

Have you attempted to work out a personal mission statement—one that transcends your present leadership position, for that matter, any leadership position? I regret to say I was in my forties before I first attempted to articulate my own unique sense of mission. The refinement of my capacity to articulate my unique mission has evolved over time, but there is amazing confluence over the nearly two decades during which I have revisited the effort on a regular basis. Here's the current version: *To multiply and accelerate the spiritual, intellectual, and professional formation and fruitfulness of leaders involved in fulfilling Christ's Great Commission.* With increasing reliability, this personal mission statement, shared with and jointly interpreted by my most committed friends, serves as a filter for potential roles and proliferating requests. It was the basis upon which I accepted my current leadership role. It continues to serve well when consulted as a compass within the challenging and multifaceted demands within and outside my organizational employment.

A sense of centeredness is also reflected in frequent self-checks against ulterior motives. Patrick Lencioni's *The Five Temptations of a CEO*[16] is an instructive parable about the role misplaced motives play when leaders lose their way. What causes leaders to lose their way? Bill George answers:

Before people take on leadership roles, they should first ask themselves two fundamental questions: "What motivates me to lead?"and "What is the purpose of my leadership?" If honest answers to the first question are simply power, prestige and money, leaders ... tend to look to other people for satisfaction and acknowledgment of their status... Leaders who focus on external gratification instead of inner satisfaction find it difficult to stay grounded. They reject the honest critic who holds a mirror to their face and speaks the truth. Instead, they surround themselves with supporters telling them what they want to hear. Over time, they lose their capacity for honest dialogue, and people learn not to confront them.[17]

Christian leaders are not immune to such ulterior motives. Otherwise, why would Peter write to first century church elders, "Be shepherds of God's flock that is under your care, watching over them—not because you must, but because you are willing, as God wants you to be; not pursuing dishonest gain, but eager to serve ..." (I Pet. 5:2). The longer I serve in leadership, the more I recognize how insidiously such motives lurk beneath the surface of every leader's soul.

Accessibility. A fourth way in which a leader's *being* exerts influence is what I call accessibility. I don't mean open door policy, although that often serves well as a symbol for healthy openness between leaders and subordinates. I might have said accountability. That is the more familiar term. But accountability only works to the extent that leaders grant the Lord, themselves, and others *access* to their souls. This has taken me a long time to understand.

Leaders' accessibility begins in their relationship with God. John calls this "walking in the light" (see I Jn. 1:5-9). Spiritual authenticity is not validated by moral perfection. On the contrary, it is validated by confession! Leaders practice attention to the kind of honesty before God that wages war with our natural impulse to fill, hide, and cover.[18] I confess to you that for me this remains a lifelong struggle. Don't ask me why. It's not as if my Father doesn't already know every one of my overt and covert attempts to fill, hide and cover. What folly for me and my leadership when I fail to embrace this discipline wholeheartedly.

Incarnational leaders also develop the discipline of self-awareness. Daniel Goleman's extensively validated research concerning *emotional intelligence* includes the idea of self-awareness.[19] Emotionally intelligent leaders systematically grant themselves access to themselves. A self-aware leader, among other things, possesses the following capacities in growing measure:

- ability to recognize and read one's emotions and emotional health;[20]
- self-perception that corresponds to a high degree with reality and squares with others' perceptions;
- realistic sense of one's own worth and capabilities.[21]

Finally, leaders take initiative to ensure that they are accessible to others. Speaking of what he calls, *Incarnate Leadership,*[22] Bill Robinson warns of the pedestal mentality when it comes to leaders' commitment to grant others access to themselves:

> Like many ministry leaders, I am in a line of work
> that encourages "being above" more than "being
> with." ... Climb on a pedestal; create more distance
> from those I'm supposed to lead. In other words,

I should grab more of what I already have at the expense of the one thing I don't have—authentic peer-to-peer relationships... We have to make a deliberate choice. We have to be intentional in resisting the forces that create gaps between ourselves and those we have been called to lead.

Counselors use the *Johari Window* (see fig. 2.2) as a means of portraying the full landscape of true accessibility. Using a four-quadrant matrix, the Johari Window illustrates that things that are true of us fall into four categories: known to self, but unknown to others (our secrets); known to others, but not to ourselves (our blind spots); known to both ourselves and others (mutually acknowledged growth needs), and known neither to ourselves nor others (the thoughts and intents of the heart that the only Scripture's two-edged sword can awaken by God's grace). Too often, leaders deny themselves and their friends access to even the "known-known" quadrant, seriously subverting leadership's *incarnational* impact.

The Johari Window

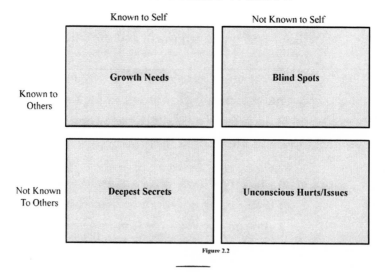

Figure 2.2

<u>Growth</u>. Stagnant leaders are suffocating leaders. Conversely, leaders exercise profound *incarnational* influence when they are growing. Steven Covey dubbed this the habit of "sharpening the saw."[23] Reggie McNeal calls it "the discipline of self-development."[24] Robert Clinton studied and taught leadership and leadership emergence over a long career at Fuller Seminary's School of Intercultural Studies. His extensive research concerning leaders who finish well reveals that lifelong learning and development consistently surfaces as a key attribute of "long haul" leaders.[25]

One of my biggest heroes and mentors in this regard is former Columbia International University Provost, Terry Hulbert. Stepping aside from executive leadership as he approached his 70s, Terry taught seminary Bible survey and geography courses full time. Having taught such courses as Pentateuch and Life of Christ for nearly 40 years, you might expect he would rely on his voluminous notes, encyclopedic memory, and trusted lecture methods. Not Terry Hulbert. As Provost, Terry recognized the significance of the emergence of information technology and invested heavily in it. Subsequently, as a full time teacher, Terry became one of our faculty's earliest and most ardent adopters of information technology. Working with an IT specialist, he created a dazzling array of Bible geography and Bible study media resources. Now in his eighties and carrying a diminished teaching load, Terry still devours resources relevant to his teaching and other wide ranging interests and generates, revises, and upgrades instructional media resources. No one should be surprised that his *incarnational* imprint deepens.

Leaders take inventory of their growth needs. They commit substantial time and resources to their personal and professional growth. They read widely, but with mission-driven focus and efficiency.[26] They deliberately seek mentors and invite comprehensive assessment of their person and performance. They embrace what Jim Collins calls "technology accelerators" for themselves and their organizations.[27] When leaders do these things, their *incarnation* of a bent toward growth will invariably infect their colleagues and accelerate their leadership success.

Grace. Above all, godly leaders paint in the *incarnational* leadership hue when they demonstrate, in the words of hymn writer Robert Robinson, "Oh to grace how great a debtor daily I'm constrained to be!" The notion that leadership means never having to say you're sorry has no place in the work of God. Leaders who are reluctant to extend grace have become too distant from and too oblivious to the grace they have received. As mentioned in the previous chapter, Jesus' extended discourse on spiritual greatness includes substantial teaching on the priority and posture of extending and receiving forgiveness.

The refrain, "There is none like you!" reverberates throughout Scripture. In many cases, the speaker refers to God's infinite power and majesty. Often, however, the reference is to God's incomparable grace. The Lord declares, "As the heavens are higher than the earth, so are my ways higher than your ways, and my thoughts than your thoughts" (Isa. 55:9). In what way do God's ways so profoundly differ from ours? He is outrageous in his forgiveness! The preceding verses invite us to: "Seek the LORD while he may be found; call on him while he is near. Let the wicked forsake their ways and the unrighteous their thoughts. Let them turn to the LORD, and he will have mercy on him, and to our God, for he will freely pardon" (Isa. 55:6-8).

Incarnational leadership involves daily appropriation, fresh testimony, and lavish imitation of the God of grace. Gracious leaders are nothing more than grace-conscious leaders. And grace is a beautiful color indeed.

Chapter Three

Primary Color #2:
***Relational** Leadership*

A second primary color in the leader's palette is *relational* leadership. Leaders lead through authentic relationships much more than through issuing directives and implementing organizational schemes. Regrettably, far too many leaders fail to paint much in this color, or apply it so thinly that it is virtually untraceable in their work. Leadership does involve the implementation of certain techniques and skills. Gifted people and others who work hard to acquire and perfect leadership skills can exercise many leadership techniques with finesse and surprising effect. But leadership that minimizes or circumvents relationship demeans people and short-circuits success. Kouzes and Posner report that their long term research has intensified their persuasion to prize the value of the *relational* aspect of leadership. They write:

> In talking to leaders and reading their cases, there
> was a very clear message that wove itself throughout

every situation and every action: *leadership is a relationship*. Leadership is a relationship between those who aspire to lead and those who choose to follow... Success in leadership, success in business, and success in life has been, is now, and will continue to be a function of how well people work and play together.[28]

Paul Hersey and Ken Blanchard[29] spearheaded one of the most widely heralded early efforts to apply social science research to the study of leadership. They formulated a "situational leadership" conceptual framework with which a great deal of subsequent research and theory has interacted. The original Hersey-Blanchard research effort explored leadership from the standpoint of two differential leader orientations: task and relationship. Conventional thinking regarded the task-relationship dynamic as a continuum. A leader's behavior would reflect a tendency toward either task behavior or relationship behavior. This was thought to be a "zero-sum" game. In other words, the more task-oriented the leader, the less it is possible, consequently, to have a relational orientation—and vice versa. Hersey and Blanchard demonstrated that task-relationship is not a zero-sum game. In fact, it is possible for leaders to exhibit *both* high task and high relationship orientation. They theorize that the optimal mix of task and relationship behavior varies with the situation. We will re-visit their research when we consider the primary color of *situational* leadership in chapter seven. The point here is that there is no inherent conflict between a commitment to getting things done and relating to people. Evidence from decades of subsequent social science research overwhelmingly substantiates that the most effective leaders are those who refuse to accept the notion that relationships are the price of getting things done.

Relational Health. What makes for a relationship? How do relationships develop and deepen? What is the pathology of relationship problems? Michael Schluter and his colleagues at the Relationships Foundation (www.relationshipsfoundation.org) have devoted themselves to deep, biblically-rooted studying of these questions, generating ideas, and advocating for improved relational health among political, academic, business, and community leaders. Schluter believes that many social, political and business problems are often far more fundamentally relational than ideological. Schluter and his colleagues have insightfully developed and validated the following five-dimensional conceptual relationships framework:[30]

- Directness – the degree and type of contact between people
- Continuity – the development of a shared story
- Multiplexity – the extent to which we know each other
- Parity – the allocation of power and respect
- Commonality – the degree of collaboration and partnership

The *Relational Health Audit* (available at www.teamfocus.co.uk) is a 30-item inventory developed by Schluter and his associates by which any personal or organizational relationship may be assessed. I have employed the *Relational Health Audit* with various relationships in view and found it offers significant insight for both diagnosing problems and mapping paths toward resolution.

Relational Ethics. There are definitely such things as relationship wrongs. The Bible speaks extensively of relational obligations and violations. Even the Ten Commandments should be understood as relational in character. Exodus 20 begins, "I am the LORD your God who brought you out of Egypt," implying that what he is about to say constitutes the basis upon which his people's relationship with him and each other should be conducted. Relationship wrongs include parental disrespect, killing, adultery, stealing and coveting. Jesus made it clear that each of these sins has insidious root forms, for example, hatred for murder, lust for adultery. But it doesn't have to be complicated. Jesus summarized the Law's relational obligations by saying, "… do to others what you would have them do to you" (Mt. 7:12). The New Testament's litany of "one another" commands serves as an additional source of guidance. Moral and spiritual values define many aspects of relationship. Many other relationship dynamics, however, are a matter of style.

Relational Style. Effective *relational* leadership begins with understanding of one's own relational style and recognition that theirs is neither the only one nor the only appropriate one. The *Social Styles* matrix (see Fig. 3.1) serves as one well-established mechanism by which to portray relational style. This matrix, first postulated in the 1960s by Dr. James Taylor, expands upon previous work by Blake and Mouton.[31] Three assessment scales contribute to the designation of a social style: (a) Assertiveness – the degree to which a person attempts to influence the thinking and action of others; (b) Responsiveness – the extent to which a person readily displays feeling when another attempts influence their thinking or action; and (c) Versatility – the extent of a person's inclination to make working relationships mutually productive. A person's social style may, thus, be characterized relative to the degree of "telling" vs. "asking" and "controlling" vs. "emoting" tendencies. The four response quadrants represent four primary social styles: Driving (telling + controlling), Expressive (telling + emoting), Amiable (asking + emoting), and Analytical (asking + controlling). In his book, *Mastering the Management Buckets*, John Pearson offers the following advice concerning social styles:

Knowing your own social style and the styles of your boss, co-workers, board members, donors, family members and others is critical for long term success. There is no "best" style. Be versatile and adapt your approach to meet the needs of others—especially your boss. Investing time in charting yourself and the other members of your organization [with reference to social styles] can be of great assistance in building a team.[32]

Although certain styles may be more effective in certain situations (stay tuned for chapter six) the point here is that leaders need to be alert to the fact that people project different relational style tendencies.

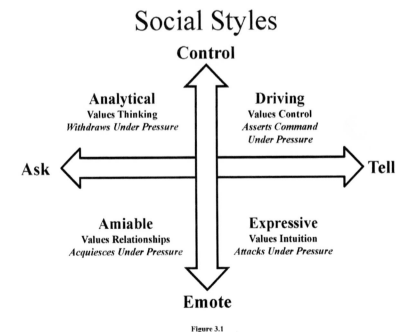

Social Styles

Control

Analytical
Values Thinking
Withdraws Under Pressure

Driving
Values Control
*Asserts Command
Under Pressure*

Ask ←———————————————→ **Tell**

Amiable
Values Relationships
Acquiesces Under Pressure

Expressive
Values Intuition
Attacks Under Pressure

Emote

Figure 3.1

Four Frames. Bolman and Deal[33] offer another way of looking at how interpersonal dynamics express themselves in organizational life. They assert that competing organizational social science theorists and management gurus both reflect existing tendencies and incline people in organizations to perceive, pursue, and attempt to resolve challenges and opportunities from the primary perspective of one of the following four frames:

- Structural – the organization exists to achieve goals efficiently; organizational problems and solutions are a function of the organizational chart, policies, procedures, norms, etc.
- Human Relations – the organization is a family; solidarity, healthy community and member care are the pathway to success.
- Political – the organization is a "jungle" in which coalitions must contend for scarce resources and competing ideas.
- Symbolic – the organization's flourishing or failure depends on the extent to which traditions, rituals, stories and other meaning-laden symbols are developed and sustained.

Bolman and Deal argue that these "frames" function both positively and negatively as alternative windows, filtering people's view of the realities before them. People tend to operate from within a primary "default" frame and, perhaps, a secondary frame. They see clearly the organization's purposes, define its problems, and propose resolution from within the limited perspective and options their "frame" affords. When there is a clash of frames, relational conflict may arise and escalate.

I'll never forget my first exposure to "The Four Frames." I was one of the instructors at a training event for new chief academic officers. One of my colleagues presented "The Four Frames" as a useful tool for thinking about and addressing the inevitable conflicts in which deans find themselves embroiled. I thought immediately of a painful, protracted conflict I had experienced some years before with a colleague who was also a good friend. We simply could not see eye to eye. Clearly, we held different ideas on some matters. But we couldn't seem to find common ground upon which to negotiate our differences. As I listened to "The Four Frames" presentation, lights went on for me. I readily recognized that my primary frame is "structural" and my secondary, "human relations." It then dawned on me that my friend's primary frame was "political" and his secondary was "symbolic." We were each ardently and sincerely assessing problems and pursuing solutions, all the while locked into completely different frames. The realization came too late for my friend and me. We had long since gone our separate ways. I'd like to think that we might have been able to resolve our differences, or at least find a more constructive way to engage them, by knowing how our "frames" contributed to our perception of the situation and its solutions.

<u>Processing Style</u>. Processing style represents another way of looking at relational variability that I have found to be extremely instructive as a leader. The speed and manner with which we think our way through information and reach conclusions differs dramatically. Figure 3.2 shows how differences between the internal-external and rapid-slow processing style may be displayed. Some of us process information slowly, others quite rapidly. Some of us process information by verbal interaction, others by detached reflection. The resulting matrix plots four generalized processing styles: rapid-external; rapid-internal; slow-external; slow-internal.

Processing Styles

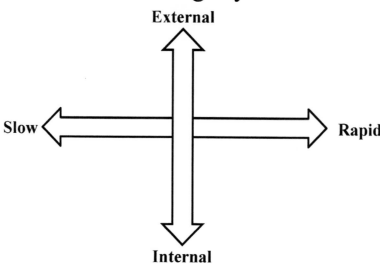

Figure 3.2

I tend to be a rapid-external processor. Rapid-external processors state their immediate grasp of the facts—or at least their tentative conclusions—since they are "thinking by talking." Leaders who are rapid-external processors may be inclined to foreclose discussion before some have had the opportunity to weigh the situation and weigh in with their wisdom and insight. On the other hand, I once served on a committee chaired by a slow-external processor who could never bring himself to discontinue discussion even when it was excruciatingly obvious to the rest of the group that it was time to decide. Slow-external processors make bad facilitators of meetings where decisions have to be reached.

Sometimes the silence of colleagues does not signal assent. It may simply mean that the internal processors have not been given adequate opportunity to reach and voice their conclusions. It is highly likely that key members of your team are slow-internal processors. I have found the following principle essential in order to invite and honor the contributions of slow-internal processor team members: *If at all possible, never discover, discuss, and decide an issue on the same occasion.* The more leaders understand their own processing style and accommodate the processing styles of others, the better the chance to preserve relational harmony and foster sound decision-making.

Relational Intentionality. It bears repeating that effective *relational* leadership begins with understanding of one's own relational style and recognition that theirs is neither the only one nor the only appropriate one. Effective leaders cultivate *awareness* of their own social, organizational, processing, and other relational style features. They *anticipate* that their colleagues' and subordinates' styles fall across the entire gamut and they actively seek to *accommodate* others' styles in the way they facilitate discussion, transact decisions, and resolve conflict. Moreover, their *accommodation* is never merely passive or grudging. They frequently signal and state that they sincerely *appreciate* the ways in which the differing styles of their team members contribute to the organization's health and success.

Teamwork. Leaders who paint brilliantly in *relational* colors do so through teamwork. They affirm the New Testament's preference for plurality in leadership. They recognize that genuine team synergy yields results that far exceed the sum individual contributions can accumulate. Sadly, too many leaders pay only lip service to teamwork. Their practices do not uphold their professions. They bail and go solo when teamwork gets tough. Team solidarity erodes and teamwork becomes a mirage.

Patrick Lencioni's, *The Five Dysfunctions of a Team*,[34] offers one of the most accurate and penetrating analyses of team dysfunction I have ever encountered. Lencioni observes that team dysfunction occurs on one or more of five levels. He portrays five symptoms of team dysfunction in pyramidal fashion (see Fig. 3.3) in order to depict the "pre-potency" of each level of dysfunction. Perhaps you remember the concept of "pre-potency" from studying Abraham Maslow's hierarchy of human needs in your introductory psychology class. If you do, you will recall that "pre-potency" refers to the idea that some human needs are more basic than others. Maslow theorized that needs on the upper level of the hierarchy (e.g., self-actualization) could not be fulfilled unless and until more fundamental needs (e.g., survival) were adequately met. Lencioni suggests the same kind of "pre-potency" exists with regard to team dysfunction. The highest levels of team functioning invariably rest upon more foundational matters. Trust stands as the base upon which all other levels of team functioning rest. How can you tell trust is absent or insufficient? Ironically, you detect it by the *lack* of intense discussion and healthy debate. A veneer of harmony on the surface of team interaction may be a symptom of underlying hostility. Dysfunction then moves to a third level: detachment. Instead of mutuality and shared commitment, it's every man (or woman) for himself. Turf gets protected, and concessions are warily negotiated. Teamwork breaks down further when peers are unwilling to subject themselves to the group's assessment of their performance. Incompetence and irresponsibility are indulged. This leads to the final stage in which the team loses any capacity to focus on results.

The Five Dysfunctions of a Team

Figure 3.3

Happily, I have observed and participated in teams where diversity of opinion and style were sought and celebrated, not merely tolerated. Heated debates were punctuated by hilarity. Friendships were deepened rather than damaged by honest differences of opinion. Individuals acted selflessly grounded upon mutual confidence that when the team won, they won. While there was substantial continuity, group solidarity functioned as a welcome mat rather than a wall for new members. *Relational* leadership fostered and sustained conditions that perpetuated these attributes and reaped the benefits for the team members and the organization.

I regret to say that I have served on teams where Lencioni's pathology of dysfunction played out like a parody in living color. The script goes something like this: The leader betrays the trust of the team and will not acknowledge it. Lively debate, peppered with good-natured ribbing, becomes a rarity. The frequency of meetings diminishes in parallel with the distaste for enduring them. Benign meetings are nothing more than a forum for issuing individual directives or ratifying deals that have already been privately negotiated. The stability of team composition disintegrates into a revolving door. Available data on individual and organizational performance is systematically ignored. The organization's malaise becomes palpable. The end is near—and it will be ugly.

Leaders who preside over team dysfunction may not be at all to blame—but they must accept responsibility and commit themselves to frank collaboration in a concerted effort to rectify the situation. Cures require accurate diagnosis and courageous intervention. If ever your team emits the dreaded symptoms of dysfunction, I recommend you consult Dr. Lencioni before it reaches the critical stage from which recovery is nearly impossible.

<u>Conflict</u>. *Relational* leadership frequently demands commitment, discernment and skill in conflict resolution. Conflict arises from many sources. In some cases, people sin against other people. They need to be confronted with humility and grace with the goal of restoration and reconciliation where possible (see, for example, Mt. 18:15-18 and Gal. 6:1). In other cases, conflict arises from differences in relational or processing style, or differences in perspective, such as we have seen above.

In still other cases, conflict arises from misunderstanding of the meaning and motives of another's actions. Wars get started over things like this. Joshua 22 chronicles the most familiar biblical example regarding conflict of this nature. Having fulfilled their obligation to remain engaged in the conquest of all of Canaan's territory, the tribes of Reuben, Gad, and the half-tribe of Manasseh were generously rewarded and gladly released to settle in their previously allocated homestead on the River Jordan's eastern side. As they traversed the river, they erected an impressive altar in order to ensure that their descendants would have a perpetual reminder of their ethnic and spiritual solidarity with their relatives on the Jordan's western side. Their western kinfolk were shocked. They took one look at the shrine and assumed it signaled apostasy! It looked to the Westerners like the Easterners were going to invite Divine retribution against the whole nation by establishing a syncretistic pagan sect. Remembering how severely God dealt with previous sacrilege (see Joshua 7), the Westerners decided they better act on the LORD's behalf lest they be punished as sympathizers. They armed themselves and marched out to confront their cousins' folly.

Things would have gotten ugly in a hurry but, thankfully, cooler heads prevailed. Before the first arrows were loosed, the Westerners sent a delegation of tribal elders to confront their Eastern counterparts, declare their provocation, and demand an explanation. The Easterners decided not to take the allegations personally. In fact, they defused the situation by agreeing that *if* the *meaning* and *motives* of their actions were indeed as they had been attributed, their counterparts' outrage would be justified. The Easterners assured their brothers they intended the exact *opposite* of what appeared to be the case and submitted themselves to Divine scrutiny and justice. When the Westerners apprehended the true motives of their Eastern cousins, they put away their weapons and called for a celebration. Just so there would be no future misunderstanding, the Easterners named the altar: "A Witness Between Us—that the LORD is God" (Josh. 22:34b).

What got this mess started? Prematurely imputing meaning and motives to another's actions. What defused it? Several things:

- direct confrontation, permitting an opportunity for the offenders to explain themselves;
- stating the outrage and the reasons for it before acting on it;
- acknowledging the validity of the offense *if* the attributed meaning and motives can be substantiated;
- ceding to God the ultimate authority and prerogative to judge when motives and meaning are in doubt.

Some years ago, Willow Creek Community Church founder, Bill Hybels, invited a highly controversial public figure to be interviewed at a public service. Some church members were outraged. How could the church give a platform to this scandalous individual? Within hours, telephone and internet lines sizzled. What did Hybels do? He called a meeting. Someone sent me the audio and I have never forgotten Bill's words or his conduct in that tense situation. In my judgment, he modeled beautifully a leader's role and disposition in conflict resolution. Bill opened the meeting by saying (I paraphrase), "one of our core Willow Creek Community Church ministry principles is that we will not allow controversy to go underground." He then gave opportunity for people to respectfully express their offense and explained the staff's motives and rationale for the invitation. The conflict subsided.

Underground conflict plagues many churches and organizations. Many leaders attempt to suppress dissent lest they be seen to countenance sinful rebellion or legitimize gossip. I do not believe this approach is usually either biblical or effective. If you don't think God permits dissent you haven't read the Psalms lately. He is sufficiently self-confident, secure, and committed to us that he will listen to even petty and groundless complaining. He doesn't justify it. He just doesn't suppress it. Once we've had our say, he will have his. When we misjudge the meaning and motives of his actions—pretty much all the time—he patiently hears our complaint and often (though not always) reveals the truth. And it works! By the time the complaint gets fully aired, the complaining Psalmist's frustration typically dissolves into trust and faith. Loyalty and submission are reaffirmed. When it comes to handling conflict and complaint, leaders could learn a lot from the Lord.

Separation. Sometimes, disagreement cannot be resolved. Despite humble, mutually respectful discussion and debate, differences of perspective, philosophy, and priorities persist. This happened to Barnabas and Paul. They were putting together a team to undertake a ministry tour to churches they had planted together. As they finalized the team roster, they couldn't agree about John Mark's inclusion. Luke tells us, "They had such a sharp disagreement that they parted company" (Acts 15:39). Note that, writing under the inspiration of the Holy Spirit, Luke does not offer an opinion as to who was right. He simply states the facts. Two godly men who had worked together fruitfully and joyfully for many years could not come to agreement about an important ministry decision. The only thing left to do was to separate.

Has that happened to you yet? If not, I expect that it will. Sometimes, separation results from sinful pride or error on the part of one or both parties. I'm not sure that was the case with Barnabas and Paul. If these things were involved, the Bible doesn't mention them. I think it is better to conclude that some disagreements result from our finiteness, not our folly. Whatever the reasons, separation occurs, even between godly leaders. The question is not whether ministry separations will occur but how we will handle them. We can do so destructively or dynamically.

The senior pastor of my beloved boyhood church had a long, fruitful ministry. He led the church to unprecedented growth in numbers, facilities, and local and worldwide Gospel impact. For reasons I do not know, the elders concluded it was time for him to step aside. He agreed—then reneged. He took it public. The elders stood their ground. People took sides. He was an icon, after all. He took lots of church members with him and started another church across town. As a young leader, I had been an ardent admirer of him. He had once invited me to serve on the church staff. I was sickened. I wrote to him, pleading that even if he had been wronged he should not allow the work God had accomplished through him to be shattered. I never heard from him. Neither church ever recovered. I returned to live in my home town several years ago. I drive by that church facility from time to time. Every time I do, I grieve. Here is a classic case of destructive separation. It doesn't have to be that way.

Was Paul and Barnabas' separation destructive? We have no evidence that it was. In fact, Scripture contains a tiny hint that it was dynamic. Writing from prison near the end of his life, Paul instructs Timothy, "Only Luke is with me. Get Mark and bring him with you, because he is helpful to me in my ministry" (2Tim. 4:11). Did Paul's ministry flourish after separating from Barnabas? By all means. He went on to dominate the New Testament narrative. What happened to Barnabas? We know very little—except that his decision not to give up on Mark was later acknowledged by Paul to have been worthwhile. If and when you have no alternative but to separate, I pray you will reap a dynamic harvest as you flee the temptation to destroy.

Predictably, some leaders are shrewd enough to recognize the correlation between relationships and success and then employ relationships as a *means* to achieving results. Closer scrutiny reveals they have little regard for relationships themselves. They invest in relationships primarily or exclusively for the purpose of realizing a return in terms of the accomplishment of their agenda. Some have called such a relational pattern *transactional*. There is an exchange in view. I relate to you only to the extent necessary to get what I want from you. The relationship amounts to little more than pretense and posturing. I have observed more than a few leaders—yes, not a few leaders of churches and Christian organizations—whose interactions with peers and subordinates is cordial, ingratiating, winsome, but ultimately superficial and manipulative. There is no true mutuality, no self-disclosure, no entrusting of oneself and little or no trust extended to others. There are some leaders with whom I have seldom, if ever, had a conversation in which I did not ultimately detect an agenda. How unbecoming of one who is called to be a *shepherd*.

Transactional relating is not only ineffective in the long run, it is ugly and unbiblical. Can you imagine discovering that the Lord Jesus' interest in you goes only so far as to recruit you to join his cause, to maneuver you into position to carry out his bidding? We are not a *means* to God's self-gratifying end. In large measure we, individually and collectively, are an inextricable *aspect* of the end toward which all his infinite ardor is devoted. Transactional relationships can't withstand the "smell" test for long. The only way transactional leaders avoid detection is to surround themselves with other transactional leaders and insulate themselves from those who show signs of picking up their scent.

The happy alternative and antidote to *transactional* relationships is *intrinsic* relationships. I relate to you not primarily because I need your cooperation to get what I want done. I relate to you because you have intrinsic value and our fellowship and collaboration beautifies and gives meaning to what we accomplish together. Leaders committed to intrinsic relationships demonstrate it by allocating resources—time, money, space—to them. They establish personal patterns and organizational rituals for cultivating and elevating individual relationships and community life.

My friend and former colleague, George Murray, planted churches in spiritually barren, Gospel-resistant northeast Italy in the 1970s. Biblically persuaded to conduct church planting by teamwork, George recruited and led a substantial team comprised of families and singles, intentionally diverse in personality and gifting. As an expression of commitment to both the people and the cause, George instituted an interesting routine. The team met twice weekly. One meeting was explicitly and (more or less) exclusively devoted to the team's church planting effort. In the other meeting, "business" was off-limits. It was a social occasion for all—couples, singles, parents, and children. Eating, playing and praying together were the order of the day. Why did they do this? George explained to me that, otherwise, "business" tended to bleed into and overtake every meeting, every conversation.

Leaders committed to intrinsic relationships will discover many ways to pursue and preserve this value. Perhaps they will differentiate between business and social interaction times, or regularly devote substantial meeting time for meaningful (not merely perfunctory) mutual engagement as persons first and colleagues second. In facility planning and allocation, they will designate and preserve valuable square footage not only with productivity in mind but also the cultivation and celebration of relationships and community. They will invest time and resources in team retreats—including spouses, if possible—and these retreats will include liberal amounts of time to *build* and *be* the team, not just transact the *business* of the team. They will withstand and overcome the resistance of those who see such things as a waste of time. They will allow themselves to be known by, not merely to know, their co-workers. Leaders who apply this primary color liberally and mix it creatively with others on the palette will create breathtaking beauty and inspire joy among those who partake of and behold it.

Chapter Four

Primary Color #3:
***Developmental** Leadership*

evelopmental leadership represents a third primary color on the leader's palette. What do I mean by *developmental* leadership? Leaders lead by identifying, developing, and releasing the giftedness of those for whom they have leadership responsibility much more than through the exercise of their own capacities, no matter how prodigious. *Developmental* leaders derive their greatest joy, not from the acclaim accorded to their personal accomplishments, but from their realization of the growth and gains their protégés have achieved. The highest form of productivity is *re*-productivity. We should pity—no, we should be grieved by—leaders who register spectacular successes for their organization only to have them subside in succeeding generations because everything revolves around them. Job One for a leader is to assemble a leadership team, shape them individually and collectively, and exercise leadership *through* that team. This is what the *shepherd* metaphor looks like in action. True shepherds do not engage in benign, static, confining oversight. They dynamically protect, actively nourish, and fruitfully nurture those under their care.

No one modeled this aspect of leadership more fully than Jesus Christ. Who can lay claim to greater capacity than he? Accessing fully the power of the Holy Spirit, he preached, healed, fed, exorcised, confronted, comforted, and even resurrected the dead. You dare not read the Gospels, however, and fail to observe that Jesus' primary leadership effort was devoted to selecting and training people to whom he would largely entrust the present and future of his divine enterprise. Few resources offer greater depth of insight into this aspect of Jesus' life than A.B. Bruce's *The Training of the Twelve*.[35] Commenting on Bruce's classic exposition, Ted Engstrom writes,

> [Bruce] suggested that the total report of the Gospels covers only thirty-three or thirty-four days of our Lord's three-and-one-half year ministry, and John records only eighteen days. What did Christ do the rest of the time? The clear implication of the Scriptures is that He was training leaders.[36]

Time and again, Jesus resolutely wrenched himself from demands and enticements that would have diverted him from this priority. He astonished his team when he disclosed that in his absence they would do even "greater things" [I take this to mean greater in scope, not in significance or substance] than he (Jn. 14:12). In a very real sense, that explains how I came to be writing this book—and how you came to be reading it. Think of it! We are the fruit of Jesus' most enduring leadership legacy.

Perhaps leaders are never more Christ-like than when they devote themselves to the work of developing a leadership team. So, how did Jesus go about developing leaders? What does *developmental* leadership entail? It should not surprise you to discover that developing people begins with selection.

Recruiting with a *Developmental* Mindset

One of the most reliable barometers of leadership I know is the capacity of a leader to recruit and retain highly capable, compatible, committed partners. When working properly, *developmental* leadership cascades throughout an organization— elevating the organization by elevating its people. It begins at the top. Show me a leader who can't assemble, develop, and keep together a core leadership team and I'll show you a leader who is in serious trouble. The systematic, discriminating manner of Jesus' key ministry partner recruitment and development is worthy of study and emulation. What characterized the people Jesus chose for senior partnership in his work? How did he go about identifying, assessing, and recruiting them? Luke describes Jesus' selection of the Twelve as follows:

> One of those days Jesus went out to a mountainside to pray, and spent the night praying to God. When morning came, he called his disciples to him and chose twelve of them, whom he also designated apostles: Simon (whom he named Peter), his brother Andrew, James, John, Philip, Bartholomew, Matthew, Thomas, James son of Alphaeus, Simon who was called the Zealot, Judas

son of James, and Judas Iscariot, who became a traitor (Lk. 6:12-16).

If you think those few verses constitute all Scripture says about Jesus' recruitment and selection process, you are sorely mistaken. It is clear that this episode represents the *culmination* of a rather lengthy process by which Jesus identified, assessed and, finally, designated his core team.

Before I offer a few observations about the criteria and process Jesus employed, I urge you not to overlook the degree to which Jesus regarded leadership team selection as profoundly consequential. Luke tells us that he, "spent the night praying to God" (Lk. 6:12b). Make a full stop there. The Son of God devotes an entire night to asking his Father for discernment in the matter of leadership team selection. How much more should we rely on the Spirit's illumination when faced with a similar undertaking? This is serious business indeed. Need I say more?

Jesus' leadership team selection process may have *culminated* in prayer, but it consisted of several other elements instructive to those of us called by him to leadership. There are several hints in the Gospels regarding the characteristics and capacities of those Jesus designated for leadership in his cause. To say that Jesus' selection criteria were unconventional is an understatement. Religious leaders in Jesus' day emerged from a lengthy, rigorous, elitist educational system. Compulsory Jewish religious education (for boys only in those days) began with *Beth Sopher* (House of Scribe). Boys between the ages of six and ten memorized the *Torah* (Genesis – Deuteronomy) under the strict and severe scrutiny of local scribes. Beginning at age 10, most boys enrolled in the more extensive *Beth Talmud* (House of Study). The boys worked through a question-answer formatted catechism of sorts and went on to memorize Psalms and Proverbs. The more diligent and endowed students destined for high status religious leadership memorized the entire Old Testament. Only the most gifted, talented, and well-connected, however, made it to the next level, *Beth Midrash* (House of Investigation). Prestige and privilege accrued to young men by their individual attachment to rabbis of distinction for this tertiary educational level. Talk about a meritocracy! The highly selective, competitive admissions process common to our most elite modern day colleges pales in comparison.

As far as we can tell, not a single one of the Twelve Jesus chose for his central leadership corps had attained religious leadership status in conventional terms. Remember how the Jewish religious and civic officials expressed disparaging astonishment that the Apostles were, "unschooled, ordinary men" (Acts 4:13)? Only Gamaliel-educated Saul (the Apostle Paul) possessed impressive elitist religious leadership credentials. Paul later eschewed his educational achievements, declaring them putrid refuse compared to the surpassing value of knowing the righteousness of Christ through faith (Phil. 3:8). As one who has earned three postsecondary degrees and invested a lifetime in formal Christian higher education, this observation gives me special pause. Conventional credentials don't count for much when it comes to essential leadership qualifications. Some years ago, I heard a report from an African brother who put it this way: *Theological education should be in the business of developing ministry leaders rather than credentialing people into the ministry.*

Apparently minimizing the conventional value placed upon intellectual prowess, knowledge, skills, and status, Jesus employed a different set of criteria. What selection criteria did Jesus appear to favor? Among others, I observe that Jesus placed high value upon three things: disposition, demonstrated capacities, and diversity.

<u>Disposition</u>. Remember I said the appointment of the Twelve recorded in Luke 6 represents the *culmination* of a much more lengthy and extensive process? Notice how the text says that, following his all-nighter in prayer, Jesus called his disciples to him and, "chose twelve [from among] them, whom he also designated apostles" (Lk. 6:12). The fishermen had long since dry-docked their boats and set aside their nets. By implication, the religious and civic officials, political activists, and others had left their occupations as well. They obeyed Jesus' summons to join his learning community (see Mt. 4:18ff; Jn. 1:37ff). They proved themselves to be disciples long before they were designated as leaders. The designation "disciple" signifies not primarily their status but their well-proven disposition to set themselves apart (i.e., to pursue holiness), follow, and learn. They had demonstrated that they were humble, reliable learners for some time.

Eligibility for leadership development should always rest upon this kind of learner's disposition. *Developmental* leadership is wasted on people who perch proudly upon and hide behind the credentials and experience platform. Leaders should look to surround themselves with *learners*, not the *learn-ed*. Leonard Sweet's whimsical *Learned to Learner Litany of Transformation*[37] captures the essence of this vital leadership disposition. Consider the following excerpts:

> *I used to be a learned professor. Now I'm a learner.*
> *When I was learned, life was a quiz show. Now that*
> *I'm a learner, life is a discovery channel...*
> *When I was learned, knowledge was everything.*
> *Now that I'm a learner, kindness is everything...*
> *When I was learned, I used to point my finger*

*and pontificate. Now that I'm a learner, I slap my
forehead all the time...*

*When I was learned, I was frightened of new ideas.
Now that I'm a learner, I'm just as frightened of
old ideas...*

*When I was learned, I knew where I was going.
Now that I'm a learner, I don't know where I'm
going—but I know who I'm going with...*

*When I was learned, I had something to teach
everybody. Now that I'm a learner, everybody has
something to teach me...*

*When I was learned, I thought that all knowledge
was a form of power. Now that I'm a learner, I
suspect much knowledge is a form of weakness.*

*When I was learned, life was knowledge about
God. Now that I'm a learner, life is knowledge
of God...*

<u>Demonstrated capacities</u>. You would be making a mistake
if you infer from Acts 4:13 that the apostles' characterization as
"unschooled, ordinary men" means they were persons of scant
capacity or accomplishment. In fact, we know that Peter, Andrew,
James and John were successful commercial fishermen. Matthew
was a civic official. We know less of the other apostles. What we do
know, however, is that we dare not regard them as inexperienced
or incompetent. Rather, they had developed and successfully
exercised life and leadership skills and demonstrated marketplace
savvy. What did Jesus look for in a potential leadership partner?
He looked for potential, to be sure. But it seems to me that he
also saw the evidence of potential in their previous real-world
exercise of life and leadership skills. I don't think Jesus engaged

in *ex nihilo* creation of leaders. There is no reason to assume the apostles constituted a raw, unformed mass of human potential. To the contrary, they give every evidence they were skilled, shrewd, socially astute and accomplished. Jesus' core leadership team members may have lacked a conventional religious leadership pedigree, but they were people of "proven potential" in terms of leadership.

Conventional recruitment and screening relies heavily upon knowledge (including formal education), skills, and experience. It often fails to account for what I believe is a much more crucial element: capacity. A former colleague had an amusing habit of peppering our conversations with management quips and quotes. The following was one of his favorites: *You can't make up in training what you lack in selection.* You cannot develop a leader out of a vacuum. What you can do is learn to recognize the scent of leadership potential wafting along the breeze of life experience. Knowledge and skills, even credentials, can be acquired. Capacity cannot. *Developmental* leaders mine for evident but untapped leadership capacity.

Diversity. At the risk of inferring too much from the New Testament text, I nevertheless think it is safe to say that one of the most remarkable features of the core leadership team Jesus assembled was its diversity. I concede that it was made up entirely of Jews, mostly Galileans, males, many of them at least distantly related to each other. Jesus worked within the framework at hand. To have done otherwise would have torn the social fabric. Nevertheless, Jesus stretched it (not a bad principle for us to observe even to this day). Within the constraints of Jesus' contemporary framework, there seems to me to be an unmistakable bias in favor of diversity. The group included, for example, men of gritty commerce (Peter, Andrew, James, John), mystical piety (Nathaniel), civil service (Matthew), and radical political dissidence (Simon the Zealot). The Gospel narrative clearly intimates wide variation in their personalities ranging from bombastic (Sons of Thunder) to reflective (Nathaniel) to mercurial (Peter) to skeptical (Thomas). We can safely assume diversity among their perspectives on many social, political, and religious issues.

I believe intentional diversity is crucial to *developmental* leadership. When sought and celebrated by a leader, diversity not only contributes strength and resilience to each individual but also distributes it throughout the entire organization. The New Testament repeatedly emphasizes that God places a high value upon unity in diversity. Jesus refers to it as the highest witness to our authenticity as his disciples (Jn. 13:35). Paul emphasizes it in his exhortations to the Roman (Rm. 12:3ff) and Corinthian (1 Cor. 12 &13) believers. Confusing uniformity with loyalty can be personally blinding and organizationally lethal. Leaders who surround themselves with sycophants and clones leave themselves and their organizations impoverished and vulnerable. I know of one organization that has gone so far as to pair each leader with a peer who is the polar opposite in personality and gifting. Weaknesses and vulnerabilities are offset by the compensatory strengths of a carefully chosen counterpart. They do this not because it is easier, but because of the toxic nature of personal insularity and the enormous dividends intentional diversity offers in terms of personal development and organizational flourishing. Whether through formal assessment or intuitive reflection, leaders should look for ways to ensure that every gift and perspective, every stakeholder connection, is represented within their leadership circle. However you go about it, I believe the case is clear that healthy diversity is an essential ingredient for the personal growth of leaders, their teams, and their organizations.

Leading with a *Developmental* Mindset

Developmental leadership is not only reflected in Jesus' approach to team selection but also in the way he led. How did he lead? I suggest we can summarize Jesus' many and diverse *developmental* strategies under two major headings: engagement and exercise.

<u>Engagement</u>. A central aspect of Jesus' designation of the Twelve, Mark tells us, is that they, "might be with him" (Mk. 3:14). Certainly this must include the notion that Jesus wanted them to stand with him. Moreover, Mark goes on to tell us that Jesus wanted them to preach and authenticate the coming of the Kingdom by confronting the demonic powers on his behalf (Mk. 3:14-15). It seems abundantly clear not only from this verse, however, but also especially from the fabric of the entire Gospel narrative, that he first and foremost beckoned the Twelve simply to be fully engaged with him.

Teamwork does not consist of distributing individual responsibility for the sake of efficiency. Teamwork involves relational, developmental mutuality. Jesus did not recruit and deploy a cadre of talented functionaries, then offload to each of them their piece of the logistical pie so that he could more fully indulge himself in activities he preferred. His company was not a collection of drones carrying out directives in neatly sealed, parallel compartments of responsibility. He called them to be *together,* to be *with* him. Don't fail to observe how thoroughly this pattern is imbedded in the fabric of the Gospel narrative.

Simply mandating individual employee growth plans, establishing corporate training curricula, and allocating professional development funding does not constitute *developmental* leadership. These provisions fully yield *developmental* results only to the extent that leaders engage deeply and personally with the team members they wish to develop. Frankly, I know far too many leaders who remain personally aloof and opaque, even among their most senior associates. Not Jesus. Jesus intentionally invited and persistently expanded his disciples' intimacy with him. During his final hours with the Twelve, he distinguishes his leadership disposition toward them from the conventional master-slave leadership dynamic familiar in both secular and religious circles. He declares, "I no longer call you servants, because a servant does not know his master's business. Instead, I have called you friends, for everything that I learned from my Father I have made known to you" (Jn. 15:15).

The extent of the apostles' engagement with Jesus afforded them comprehensive exposure to his passions, priorities, precepts, principles, motives, frustrations, enemies. Such intimacy permitted their hidden motives, fears, and secret rivalries to be exposed, their corrupt and confused understanding to be corrected, their mistakes to be manifest, their failures to be redeemed. It was messy, meandering, inefficient leadership. Or was it? When the time came for Jesus' disciples to exercise leadership that would perpetuate his redemptive agenda, they were prepared. As the Holy Spirit prompted and empowered them, they discovered the imprint of his heart and mind upon theirs. They remembered his prayerful confidence that they would succeed. They witnessed with astonishment the flowering of their gifts and capacities. By God's grace, they could do more than produce. They could *re-produce*.

Exercise. Jesus did more than model ministry and talk about ministry. He developed his disciples by giving them *exercise*. Mark makes it clear that part of Jesus' purpose in appointing the Twelve was, "that he might send them out" (Mk. 3:14). Among the many forms of *exercise* involved in *developmental* leadership, let us briefly examine two: delegation and debriefing.

Developmental leadership involves, as Kouzes and Posner put it, "enabling others to act."[38] The more conventional term is delegation. But delegation becomes developmental only when exercised in a developmental fashion. Many leaders delegate to offload trivial tasks and distasteful duties. They prefer to constrain initiative rather than to channel creativity. When that pattern is prominent in a leader, claims to *servant* leadership should be regarded with skepticism. Other leaders fail in *developmental* leadership by engaging in what my friend Hans Finzel calls "dirty delegation."[39] Dirty delegation is inefficient. It demoralizes. Worst of all, it subverts *developmental* leadership.

Dirty delegation manifests itself in two forms: ambiguity and ambivalence. Ambiguous delegation occurs when the leader fails to make clear or consistent the level of assigned authority and responsibility. Do you intend to grant full discretion for both means and results? Do you want explicit methods and procedures followed? Chances are quite high that the specific responsibility and authority you think you are delegating and what your subordinate perceives you are delegating may be seriously misaligned. *Developmental* leaders find ways to communicate clearly their intentions with regard to delegated responsibility. They anticipate ambiguity. They work to communicate explicitly and develop written protocols within which subordinates may implicitly understand the nature and extent of delegation. Good protocols encompass both major variables: authority and responsibility. When the two are misaligned or either is ambiguous, frustration and failure are likely to ensue. And *developmental* leadership becomes a casualty.

When a leader assigns a task and then overtly, covertly, or (as is more often the case) inadvertently takes it back, it exposes underlying ambivalence toward *developmental* leadership. *Developmental* leaders must not be risk averse—and they cannot be ambivalent about delegation. When they delegate, they must be prepared to release commensurate responsibility and authority and live with the results. They may suffer short term setbacks in terms of results, but they will reap long term benefits in terms of individual and organizational development. Constraints on failure are proportional to constraints on success. I don't see how you can seriously contemplate God's ways and fail to conclude that he favors the "room to fail" alternative. If you claim to be a godly leader, I recommend you regularly check your risk aversion and its telltale expression in ambivalent delegation.

Jesus' sending of his disciples had an intrinsic purpose—to announce and authenticate the coming of the Kingdom. But it clearly had a *developmental* purpose as well. How do we know? We know because he liberally delegated responsibility and authority to his disciples. We also know because he engaged in a consistent pattern of collectively debriefing their experiences. Virtually every occasion in which Jesus or his disciples exercised public ministry was followed by a private debriefing. On these occasions, the meaning of Jesus' words and actions was more fully disclosed, the mistaken notions of his disciples exposed, their failures corrected, fears and frustrations confronted. *Developmental* leaders adopt a similar pattern.

Remember my friend with the management quips? Here's another of his favorites: *There is a difference between 20 years of experience and one year of experience 20 times.* Experience is not the best teacher after all. Experience *reflected upon* is the best teacher. *Developmental* leaders latch onto every teachable moment. They take responsibility rather than laying blame. They leverage failure, frustration, confusion, surprise, disturbance, disappointment for the benefit of learning and growth.

Evaluation represents a formal means of debriefing individual performance and fostering growth. *Developmental* leaders welcome evaluation. They impose evaluation first upon themselves and their efforts and only then upon their co-workers and their efforts. To use the language of educators, they prefer *formative* (i.e., for the purpose of improving and growing the person) evaluation over *summative* (i.e., for the purpose of rating or retaining the person) evaluation. They work to foster an organizational culture of assessment and improvement. Team members learn to welcome evaluation because it is regular, fair, based upon pre-agreed mutual expectations, and provides means, opportunity, and resources for improvement and growth.

Leaders paint in the *developmental* color by gathering and growing other leaders. This is what takes leadership beyond performance and productivity to the *re*-productivity that underlies the Creator's design for your destiny and the destiny of those he has entrusted to your leadership. Make sure you apply it in ample measure, brushing the canvas of others' lives with your unique God-given flair.

Chapter Five

Primary Color #4:
***Directional** Leadership*

O ne of the boldest colors with which a leader paints is *directional* leadership. Leaders lead by helping stakeholders to clarify and coalesce around a coherent mission and compelling vision. Please don't misunderstand me. *Directional* leadership is not about leaders issuing *directives*. I have observed plenty of leaders who are not shy about giving orders. Yet, their path and that of their organization remains erratic and confused. Many such leaders latch onto a clever methodology, cater to every pressing demand, or obsess over minutiae at the expense of the mainstream. In so doing, they dissipate the energy and diminish the effectiveness of everyone involved. Such a leader may project a determined and driven demeanor, but their *directional* compass oscillates and the organization loses its way.

Mission

If you have observed anything about highly effective organizations, you know that invariably they have a clear sense of mission and their members buy into it wholeheartedly. Leaders make it a priority to help clarify the mission and to ensure that it is widely understood and wholeheartedly embraced by members. This does not mean that leaders must intuitively or independently originate and articulate the organization's mission. Some leaders are exceptionally gifted at conceptualizing. They can apprehend in crystal clear terms the organization's core purpose and express it concisely and compellingly. *Directional* leadership, however, does not require these gifts. In fact, a leader's strengths in these gifts may present challenges in terms of stakeholder buy-in.

The issue with mission is not merely the capacity to articulate it in a clever and concise manner. Rather, it is to help the organization's stakeholders to grasp and gather around the mission. Leaders must play a catalytic role, but they need not play the central role in articulating the mission. If the mission statement is handed down from on high, stakeholders may or may not own it. My colleague David Medders introduced me to this leadership aphorism: *People own what they help create.* Regardless of the clarity with which you as a leader can see and state the organization's mission, remember that is nowhere near what is required by *directional* leadership. Too often, organizational mission amounts to little more than words on a wall or a slogan on a business card. Inattentive and ineffective leaders check off that task and move on to bigger and better things—and wonder why they can't seem to get anywhere.

What makes for a good mission statement? Wrong question. The statement is less important than the substance. Don't get me wrong. I understand the sizzle is what sells the steak. How you state your mission matters. But sizzle with no steak cannot satisfy hunger or sustain interest. So, first things first: What are the key components of a well-conceived "mission"? You could spend an hour browsing the internet and come up with a dozen lists of key ingredients. For me, the substance of mission boils down to two irreducible things:

- What you do stated in terms of *enduring ends* rather than current means.
- The beneficiaries *for whom* you do what you do.

<u>Enduring ends.</u> One of the most critical aspects of understanding and articulating mission is to clarify "what business we are in." Writing in the *Harvard Business Review* in 1960, Theodore Levitt[40] may have been the first to insert this key diagnostic into the leadership lexicon. I first came across it in John Nesbitt's *Megatrends*[41] in the late 1980s. Levitt, and Nesbitt after him, cite the railroad industry as the classic example of failing to understand "what business we are in." They attribute the railroads' decline to the fact that they assumed that they were in the *railroad* business rather than, as was actually the case, the *transportation* business. When new modes of transportation supplemented and supplanted railroads, you might say industry leaders clung to the rails and got run over by the oncoming train. Nesbitt suggests that leaders in the telephone industry, on the other hand, got it right. They understood that they were in the *communications* business, not the *telephone* business. They foresaw that new technologies threatened the obsolescence of POT (plain old telephone) service. They innovated and invested in emerging technology such as cellular, digital, voice over internet, and satellite communications.

The telecommunications industry thrives. The railroad industry has rebounded slowly after awakening from the train wreck.

When I first came to the organization with which I currently serve, The Association for Biblical Higher Education, we came to recognize that we had inadvertently come to think of our mission as encompassed by its historic principle *activity*. Founded in 1947 as the Accrediting Association of Bible Colleges, the association has served as the recognized North American accrediting agency for institutions specializing in biblical and ministerial leadership education. In the 1940s, regional accreditation was inaccessible to such specialized institutions. Since the 1960s, however, more and more regional agencies have welcomed biblical higher education institutions to their ranks. Although ABHE accreditation is more rigorous, robust, and widely recognized than ever, regional accreditation remains the "coin of the realm." Many of our members now carry dual accreditation. Some who achieved regional accreditation felt ABHE accreditation was redundant and dropped their membership. If you had asked both organizational insiders and outsiders, "What business is ABHE in?" they would have reflexively answered, "That's obvious, you're in the accreditation business." We had made the classic mistake of confusing the *means* with the *mission*. Turnaround began for ABHE when we began to understand that "the business we are in" is the quality and credibility business. Accreditation represents the primary historic *means*—but perhaps not the best or only present and future means—by which we pursue our core business. These days we say our aim is not merely to be the accrediting agency our members can live with but the service and resource partner they can't live without.

Directional leaders relentlessly engage their organization's best minds to visit and re-visit the matter of *enduring ends*. Activity—even the activity that many people associate with your primary historic success—is not equivalent to mission. *Ends* are primary. Means are secondary. Mission is permanent. Means may be temporary. Leaders observe carefully and involve others in discerning the difference.

Beneficiaries. *Directional* leaders not only champion the quest to distinguish *mission* from *means,* but also they dial in a laser focus on the question of *for whom* the organization does what it does. For business leaders, this means, "Who is the customer?" The more precisely they can answer that question, the more likely they are to be successful. Many ministry leaders (perhaps too few!) are wary and uncomfortable with employing such commercial terminology to the question of *for whom* do we exist? With commendable motive, some ministry leaders simply state or imply that God is the ultimate audience or beneficiary, ensuring that mission statements include the obligatory "to the glory of God." While I heartily acknowledge that, for the Christian leader and organization, all we do must be ultimately for an audience of One—and I'll have a lot more to say about that in Chapter Eight—I don't think leaders should allow themselves to avoid the more immediate and direct question: *For whom do we do what we do?*

Several years ago, Charlie Davis, then International Director of The Evangelical Alliance Mission (TEAM), assembled a group of board members and other internal and external stakeholders to re-visit this question. Predictably, some of us balked when confronted with the question of who is TEAM's "customer." A member of our group, an attorney by profession, offered a more apt and useful framework that everyone readily embraced: the trust agreement (see Fig. 5.1). A trust agreement involves the entrustment of assets to a trustee (who sometimes engages the services of a "corporate trustee" when special expertise and guidance are required) in order that the assets' value and benefit may be conveyed to a beneficiary. This sparked a lively and fruitful discussion concerning TEAM's mission. In the end, we affirmed that the people for whose ultimate benefit TEAM exists are—not our missionaries, not churches, not financial contributors (all of whom are legitimate stakeholders)—but *lost people* (see Fig. 5.2). God has entrusted the Gospel, not to TEAM, but to the church, for the benefit of lost people.

Elements of a Trust Agreement

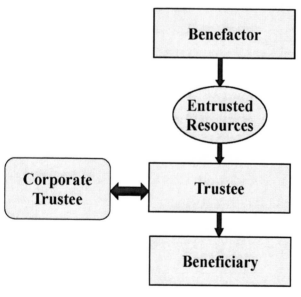

Figure 5.1

Talk about a clarifying exercise. We looked at our mission statement with new eyes. *TEAM exists to help churches send missionaries to establish reproducing churches in other lands.* We realized that, in too many ways, we had been behaving as if our mission was to *get* churches to help *us* send missionaries. Some of our missionaries assumed *they* were the ones for whose benefit our North American operations exist. What would be different if we re-aligned our missionary support services and sending systems according to this clarified understanding regarding the ones *for whom* TEAM exists? You can imagine that exercise left in its wake no small amount of discomfort as well as significant reorientation and renewal. This is the kind of thinking *directional* leaders prompt over and over again.

TEAM Trust Agreement

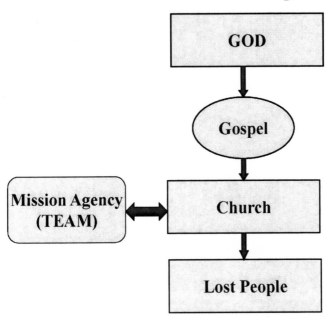

Figure 5.2

One of the underlying factors in much of contemporary church renewal reflects fresh contemplation of the *enduring ends* and *for whom* questions relative to local churches. In case you haven't noticed, churches in North America have been in serious decline for over a decade. The root of this decline is spiritual, to be sure. But why then are some churches growing exponentially? Is it simply because they have diluted the Gospel and are pandering a sugary substitute to a superficial, gullible audience? Doubtless this is true in some cases. But in many other cases, I believe church leaders have taken sober inventory of traditional *church programs* and developed new *means* for achieving the church's *enduring ends*. They have asked themselves and their members anew *for whom* the church exists. Of course, the church exists for the benefit of believers. But serious stagnation soon afflicts a church with a primarily inward orientation. When churches recognize that they are the *means* through which the Kingdom message is preached and authenticated to a dying world, they thrive. Activities are altered. Priorities are realigned. People far from God are redeemed. Churches are renewed. Why? Because leaders have helped members to revisit the mission and, where necessary, recast it in terms of these two key questions.

<u>Crafting a Mission Statement</u>. Before we move on, let's talk about the sizzle. Mission substance is more important than mission statement. But the statement matters. Too often, mission statements resemble the proverbial definition of a camel: a horse designed by a committee. They are lengthy and laborious, ponderous and pedestrian. Good mission statements are distinguished by their brevity and simplicity. They employ strong active verbs that zero in on the *effects* you intend to achieve rather than capturing the circumference of your *efforts*. They lend themselves to easy memorization and recitation. Some would say if a ten-year-old can't remember and recite it easily, the mission statement is destined for oblivion. Above all, mission statements should inspire as much as they inform. In his book *Axiom*, Bill Hybels writes about why language matters as follows:

The very best leaders I know wrestle with words until they are able to communicate their big ideas in a way that captures the imagination, catalyzes action, and lifts spirits. They coin creeds and fashion slogans and create rallying cries, all because they understand that language matters... Choose the right words and you'll set up everyone you lead for a level of effectiveness you never thought could be achieved.[42]

Vision

Mission and vision go together. Mission without vision can be sterile and stifling, if not onerous. Vision captures the imagination and sustains the soul of a people. Mission is about definition and duty. Vision is about direction and destiny. People want to follow a leader who can articulate vision. In their research on what kind of a leader people are eager to follow, Kouzes and Posner document that "forward looking" is the second most desirable leader characteristic (after "walks the talk," as mentioned in chapter two). They write, "Compelling visions distinguish credible leaders from other credible individuals."[43] *Directional* leaders do so not so much as uniquely sagacious seers, but by engaging in dialogue with others about what they see across the next horizon.

What is vision? Brace yourself for more alliteration: *Vision is an insightful ... inspiring ... image-rich ... invitation ... to partners' identification ... involvement ... and investment... in an imagined future* (see Fig. 5.3). Vision offers insight—a clarifying set of lenses through which to see the present and project the future. Vision is not vision if it does not inspire. Vision works best when it is rich in imagery. Some have defined vision as, "a picture of an imagined future that inspires passion." If you're inclined to left-brained logic, you're going to need to enlist some of your right-brained friends to help create a vivid picture.

Vision is ...

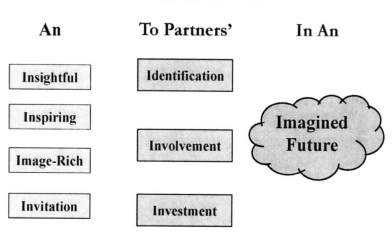

Figure 5.3

Above all, vision is more than a projection, it is an implicit *invitation*. Studying and pondering this topic a few years ago, this *invitation* aspect of vision struck me like a thunderbolt. The greatest visionary of all is God himself. Think about it. When he created the world, he didn't so much create a finished product as he generated a vast, vibrant, vivid creative project. He has invited us humans to participate with him in bringing about the full and exquisite extent of its potential. He said to Adam and Eve, "Be fruitful and increase in number; fill the earth and subdue it. Rule over the fish in the sea and the birds in the sky and over every living creature that moves on the ground" (Gen. 1:28). He didn't say merely, "Sit back and watch what I will perform." He *invited* the first couple and their progeny to contribute their own imagination, passion, and creativity to the effort.

Leadership is not about wrenching a grudging effort out of virtual slaves or grandstanding for adoring spectators. It is about inviting partners to identify with and participate in bringing about something worth giving your life for. When people sign up for a vision, everything they have comes with it. You don't have to wrangle their resources out of them. Resources follow vision. You don't have to plead for their loyalty or time. They are eager to invest. They line up to be involved.

We all know Adam and Eve blew the opportunity. They subverted God's grand invitation by succumbing to the adversary's bogus offer to control and take credit for the entire project. But the vision didn't end there. God didn't give up. Listen anew to these excerpts of the vision into which he has invited us to participate with him with redeemed ardor and creativity:

> Then I saw "a new heaven and a new earth," for the first heaven and the first earth had passed away, and there was no longer any sea. I saw the Holy City, the new Jerusalem, coming down out of heaven from God, prepared as a bride beautifully dressed for her husband. And I heard a loud voice from the throne saying, "Look, God's dwelling place is now among the people, and he will dwell with them. They will be his people, and God himself will be with them and be their God. 'He will wipe every tear from their eyes. There will be no more death' or mourning or crying or pain, for the old order of things has passed away." He who was seated on the throne said, "I am making everything new!" ... And he carried me away in the Spirit to a mountain great and high,

and showed me the Holy City, Jerusalem, coming down out of heaven from God. It shone with the glory of God, and its brilliance was like that of a very precious jewel, like a jasper, clear as crystal… I did not see a temple in the city, because the Lord God Almighty and the Lamb are its temple. The city does not need the sun or the moon to shine on it, for the glory of God gives it light, and the Lamb is its lamp. The nations will walk by its light, and the kings of the earth will bring their splendor into it. On no day will its gates ever be shut, for there will be no night there. The glory and honor of the nations will be brought into it. Nothing impure will ever enter it, nor will anyone who does what is shameful or deceitful, but only those whose names are written in the Lamb's book of life. Then the angel showed me the river of the water of life, as clear as crystal, flowing from the throne of God and of the Lamb down the middle of the great street of the city. On each side of the river stood the tree of life, bearing twelve crops of fruit, yielding its fruit every month. And the leaves of the tree are for the healing of the nations. No longer will there be any curse. The throne of God and of the Lamb will be in the city, and his servants will serve him. They will see his face, and his name will be on their foreheads. There will be no more night. They will not need the light of a lamp or the light of the sun, for the Lord God will give them light. And they will reign for ever and ever. (Rev. 21:1 - 22:5, excerpted)

Even when all that comes to pass, it will only be a new beginning in the eternal creative partnership. Are you weeping yet? Want to sign up all over again? That's what vision is all about. And that's what godly, *directional* leaders will seek to emulate, however haltingly.

Reinforcement

Directional leadership involves more than crafting mission and vision. The following leadership aphorism is attributed to Steven Covey: "The main thing is to keep the main thing the main thing." The "main thing" involves conveying mission and vision persuasively to everyone affected, time after time. People move in and out of the organization. Leaders are "talking to a parade." Moreover, "vision leaks," says Bill Hybels.[44] People have lives. They get distracted. Leaders know this and they make mission and vision a central part of every leadership conversation.

Few things convey mission and vision more powerfully than story-telling. My friend Anthony Bell offers the following insight into the importance of story-telling for leaders:

> Imagine you join your friends one evening to watch a movie you've never seen ... only you've stayed late at the office and arrive late. They briefly and barely acknowledge your presence, their eyes still transfixed to the screen. Your gaze follows theirs, and captured by the tensions, intrigued by the scene, and caught up with the characters, you squeeze into whatever space is left on the couch. You've joined the story.
>
> But you have a ton of questions. Who are the

good guys and who are the bad guys? What's happened so far? Where did it all begin? What's the big threat? Why is the guy in the blue shirt so anxious? In the absence of answers, you begin making assumptions, so that the story as you are experiencing it can make sense. But at the back of your mind, you have this nagging feeling that you have the story wrong, that your assumptions are wrong. So you sit back, experience the scenes, and little more. You have no context. You don't know the story.

So it is when someone joins a new organization. Almost invariably, they land in the middle of the story, and they don't know what's going on. Who are the good guys? Who are the bad guys? Why is the head of such-and-such a department (the one in the blue shirt) so anxious? This is where great leaders step in. They tell you the story. They hit the pause button on the remote, and they give you the details of the plot. They tell you what's happened so far and what's led up to the scene you've landed in. No wonder, you realize, the guy in the blue shirt is so worried.

But great leaders do more than that. They not only tell you what's happened so far, they consciously bring you into the story. You're no longer watching the movie, you're *in* the movie. You're a bona fide character with a role to play. And great leaders will tell you how they hope the story will work out, and more than that, they'll make it clear why your role is so important. "We can't get there without you," they'll tell you. "That's why we called on you. We wrote your character into the story because we're not sure we can make it without you. Help us write this story so that it ends well." That kind of initiation, you might guess, is uncommon and unusual. More often than not, instead of a story, you're given a manual, whether real or metaphoric: here's *what* you do and here's *how* you do it. Great leaders don't ignore the what and the how, but they add the *why* and the *where*: why it's important and where it will get us. They are not just story tellers; they are story makers.[45]

Alignment

Directional leaders don't just see that mission and vision have been crafted and communicated. They work to make sure every aspect of the organization is properly aligned with mission and vision. Policies and procedures won't get the job done. Jim Collins writes, "Executives spend too much time drafting, wordsmithing, and redrafting vision statements, mission statements, values statements, purpose statements, aspiration statements, and so on. They spend nowhere near enough time trying to align their organizations with the values and visions already in place."[46] Alignment ultimately proceeds from two key leadership responsibilities: people and planning.

Alignment Through People. In his heralded research concerning how a few companies make and sustain the leap from *Good to Great*,[47] Jim Collins documents that great companies distinguish themselves by getting "the right people on the bus, the wrong people off the bus, and the right people in the right seats on the bus." *Directional* leaders successfully recruit and deploy other leaders and work to configure a role for each team member that optimizes their contribution to the organization's mission and vision. They also act promptly and boldly—with godly forbearance but resolute firmness—to remove or redeploy employees, volunteers, donors, even board members (by all means acting in concert with board policies) who will not or cannot align themselves with mission and vision. Failure to redeploy misaligned people demoralizes other committed partners and ultimately derails the organization.

There are at least four general grounds for redeploying people within or away from the organization:

- Conduct – The person seriously or repeatedly violates clear moral or organizational standards.
- Compatibility – The person cannot or will not assimilate into team chemistry or embrace organizational culture.
- Competence – The person's performance fails to meet expectations, even after formative evaluation and opportunity for improvement.
- Capacity – The person's performance in a given role has been satisfactory in the past, but present or future demands exceed their capacity. This category requires the most discerning assessment and careful shepherding.

I have had both painful and happy experiences redeploying people. I have helped to move some reluctant people to new roles in which they flourished. Some still thank me over and over. On the other hand, I have had to bear acute misunderstanding and virulent resentment from some who could not accept the judgment of myself and others that they did not fit. Redeploying people should cause a leader pain. In fact, in many ways, leadership is a form of pain-bearing.[48] In his famous toothache comedy monologue Bill Cosby joked, "Novocain doesn't kill pain; it merely postpones it." Failing to redeploy works the same way. It doesn't eliminate pain. It postpones, intensifies, and spreads it. *Directional* leaders will pay attention to and absorb the pain for optimal people alignment.

Alignment Through Planning. Aspiration and articulation do not accomplish mission and vision. Without planning, mission and vision dissipate. This is not a book about how to plan. There are plenty of planning schemes and methods available. Experiment with planning methods and frameworks. Find one that works for you. As you do so, however, keep in mind that effective alignment through planning requires *directional* leaders to exercise steadfastly two essential planning disciplines: *plan strategically* and *plan sparingly*.

Plan strategically. Many plans fail because they do not account for the broader context in which the organization exists. No amount of planning to improve railroad transportation could overcome the crushing strategic reality that faster and more flexible modes of transportation had emerged. As Einstein put it so familiarly, insanity is doing the same thing over and over again and expecting different results. There are problems and there are facts of life. Leaders learn to tell the difference. Strategic planning calls for looking at the emerging opportunities and looming obstacles that may be game changers for your organization: Are you sure you have accurately named the business you are in? It requires you to re-examine and re-validate the "value proposition" between you and your key stakeholders: Do they still need and value what you are doing?

Strategic planning requires you to have the right people at the table. It calls for those right-brained intuitive people to dominate the mix. It emerges from strategic thinking, not from rigidly following the recipe in the latest "ten steps of strategic planning" cookbook. Leaders know that tactical planning (designating the key means by which we will accomplish our intentions) and operational planning (the projected path, timetable and resources required to accomplish our intentions) are subordinate and subsequent to strategic planning. *Directional* leaders don't fail to think and plan strategically.

Plan sparingly. Plans also fail because they are too bulky. Good planning is participatory. Especially at the operational level, it should flow up from the grass roots. It requires the input of all major stakeholders and systems. But good planning is not the accumulation of everyone's aspirations. Ultimately, a plan represents the *elimination* of options. *Directional* leadership has every bit as much to do with helping to determine what an organization is *not* called to do as it does with what it *is* called to do. Craig Groeschel writes, "Instead of thinking about what to add to your ministry to-do list, perhaps you should pray about what to add to your ministry to-don't list."[49] I have seen many organizations falter and flounder because leaders did not have the courage to say no, to *plan sparingly*.

Directional leadership is not the base color on the leader's palette. Leaders don't merely set direction and issue orders. They influence through their being and their relationships. They lead by helping people to grow and flourish. But they also know that leadership involves direction, movement, concert and economy of effort. So they exercise *directional* leadership by fostering processes to ascertain mission and articulate vision and by aligning people and plans accordingly. This color is required if the images on your leadership canvas are going to take shape.

Chapter Six

Primary Color #5:
Ecological Leadership

Perhaps the most subtle color on the leader's palette is *ecological* leadership. Leaders lead by exercising environmental sensitivity and skill: nurturing a community identity, engendering and espousing shared values, and cultivating a wholesome organizational climate. They understand that the success of their efforts may depend heavily upon their ability to read the signals of culture and climate and foster conditions that permit prospering and productivity. They recognize that talent, technique and tenacity seldom overcome toxicity.

I was originally writing this chapter during the 2010 FIFA World Cup competition in South Africa. Perennial soccer powers France and England had been eliminated in embarrassing fashion. France did not make it out of group play, failing to win a single game. England was humiliated by Germany in the so-called "knock-out" round of 16 teams. To say the French and English sides did not live up to expectations is an understatement. Both teams were loaded with world class talent. They had legendary coaches. They were expected to be serious contenders. They both fell flat. Why? Evidence indicates that the culture and climate of both teams was ravaged by infection. Dissension simmered. Pettiness proliferated. Solidarity splintered. Tabloids tattled. It got ugly. Neither of the coaches, and few of the players, would survive the ignominy.

Organizational Culture

Discerning Values. My studies and experiences in leadership do not qualify me to write extensively about cross-cultural leadership. I acknowledge that, despite my commitment to grapple deeply with biblical principles and objectively assert their applicability to many cultures, my views of leadership are heavily influenced by my American cultural identity and leadership experiences. If you are leading in an intercultural context, I strongly recommend you digest my friend James Plueddemann's highly insightful book, *Leading Across Cultures: Effective Ministry and Mission in the Global Church.*[50]

I know enough about culture, however, to insist that cultural lenses and cultural sensitivity are essential even when leaders are working *within* their native cultures. In fact, familiarity with their home culture may blind leaders to the necessity of recognizing the potentially volatile interactions between their own "assumed, hidden, subtle, and unspoken"[51] internal values and the individual and collective values entrenched within the organizations they are called to lead. Just as societies have cultures, organizations also have cultures. These cultures may be laden with unwitting and undesirable ways which nevertheless act as powerful conforming agents. Beneath the surface of everyday interactions, the "iceberg" of culture dictates what the organization's members regard to be important and how they should comport themselves. In general, the older the organization, the more deeply and powerfully the framework of organizational culture embeds itself.

Leaders ignore culture at their peril. Too often, new leaders joining an organization from the outside fail to approach the situation in a cross-cultural posture. Instead of listening, looking, and learning, they interpret for themselves the meaning and value of existing organizational patterns, rituals, and symbols, prematurely subjecting them to question and ridicule. They seek to impose their own patterns, rituals, and symbols upon an increasingly offended and suspicious community. When the intra-cultural gap is wide, the ensuing clash frequently renders casualties of the new leader, key long term subordinates, or both.

Developing Values. When leaders have taken the time to observe and learn existing organizational culture, they have won the right to help refine and reshape organizational culture. Successful organizations are held together by a powerful cultural fabric that serves as a flag for members and a banner by which they are known to outsiders. Organizational culture rests upon values—often more implicit than explicit—which are expressed and perpetuated by rituals and symbols. Mission answers the *who, what, why* questions; values answer the *how* question. Mission sets boundaries regarding *ends*; values set boundaries regarding *methods* and *means*. Values serve as a kind of shorthand for, "this is the way we do things around here." They shape reflexive, gut level[52] responses to matters such as the following:

- What (or who) is most important within our organization?
- What kinds of initiative are likely to be rewarded (or punished)?

- What should we do when we encounter disagreements or conflicts?
- What are we committed to preserving at all costs, regardless of changing external circumstances?
- How (or even when) may I decide to act in the absence of explicit instructions?
- How and to what extent should dissent be expressed?
- What makes people more or less valuable team members?

When it comes to assigning meaning and value to behavior, rituals and symbols always trump rhetoric and slogans. John Pearson illustrates:

> What happens when team members who don't walk the talk line their walls with your plaques and awards? What do reserved parking spaces communicate to your employees, customers, and visitors?
>
> **THIS PARKING SPACE IS RESERVED FOR HIS HIGHNESS, OUR CEO.**
>
> Is your leadership group named the "Management Council," the "Management Team," or the "Leadership Cabinet"? Does it matter? Why do people leave your organization? Do you ask them? Are they honest? When you announce the next great idea, are naysayers valued or quieted? Is there a trash can underneath the bottomless suggestion box?[53]

Ecological leadership involves helping community members to review and renew the mutual commitments that make up organizational culture. I have on several occasions found the approach illustrated in Fig. 6.1 to be useful in examining and reformulating organizational values. Through polling or, preferably, focus groups, ask people to identify values in three categories: stated values, actual values, and preferred values. *Stated values* would include any existing core values statements as well as any values explicitly reflected in official organizational documents such as principles, policies, and procedures. *Actual values* represent respondents' perception of how "the vast majority of people act the vast majority of the time" within your organizational context. In my experience, participants often discover stark and disconcerting dissonance between stated and actual values. As is the case with all deep learning, experiences of dissonance provide fresh motivation to clarify values. *Preferred values* represent respondents' opinion as to what core values should be formally articulated and championed throughout the organization.

Values Development Matrix

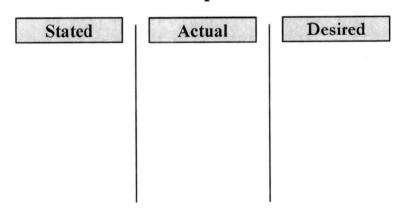

Stated	Actual	Desired

Figure 6.1

Ecological leaders work with key stakeholders to develop a set of no more than three to six core values that will serve as a compass by which to reliably guide behavior, priorities, and policies. They lead in courageous self-examination of organizational rituals and symbols. They assess the implicit values these rituals and symbols express and the degree of concurrence between implicit and explicit values. They subject themselves and others to sober assessment of the degree to which members emulate core values. They discard dissonant rituals and symbols and institute new ones that help to align conduct with commitments. They "call fouls,"[54] as Bill Hybels puts it, on themselves and others when core values are violated. They act respectfully but resolutely to discipline or remove members who refuse by active or passive opposition to conform.

Organizational Climate

In addition to discerning and developing organizational culture, *ecological* leadership involves sensing and seeding organizational climate. Organizational climate consists of implications of the collective perceptions of an organization's members upon their motivation and performance. Although the terms culture and climate are used somewhat interchangeably in research and professional literature, I believe the distinction merits maintaining. Behavior reveals culture. Perception reveals climate. Culture is about what people *do*. Climate is about how people *feel*. Organizations with relatively well-defined cultures can nevertheless register poor climate conditions.

The relativity and volatility of perception is easy to illustrate from my marriage. Precisely the same temperature conditions are invariably perceived by me to be too cold and by my wife to be too hot—and sometimes, vice versa! Moreover, sometimes I feel cold at 72 degrees and sometimes I feel hot at 72 degrees. No change in temperature has occurred. But the change in perception matters to me! When I feel too cold or too hot, my discomfort distracts me from other occupations. When the discomfort is substantial, it preoccupies me regardless of how determined I may be to ignore it.

Organizational climate operates in much the same way. Actual conditions may be identical, but perceptions may vacillate, resulting in preoccupation and de-motivation. Leaders who ignore substantial or persistent changes in organizational climate or misapprehend the underlying perceptual conditions may pay a high personal and organizational price. Insisting that perception is irrational and unpredictable does not diminish its motivational and performance implications.

Sensing Climate. Leaders too often miss organizational climate change signals. *Ecological* leaders develop internal or external gauges by which to assess and optimize their co-workers' satisfaction and motivation. They do this both because they care about their co-workers and also because they know that perception—even false perception—issues in real consequences. Some leaders possess high levels of intuition relative to climate. Others must invite trusted advisors to help them recognize critical perception changes. Babbes and Zigarelli[55] suggest that leaders need to designate something (or someone) akin to the canary in a coal mine. Regular assessment of the workplace environment, such as that offered by *Best Christian Workplaces Institute,*[56] or the *Team Climate Inventory,*[57] for example, should supplement more objective measures of organizational productivity and performance.

Seeding Climate. Leaders need not be passive about climate. They can be proactive. They can relentlessly employ personal practices and instill organizational rituals and rewards intended to enhance their team's perception of the value of their contributions. When climate deterioration is detected, however, leaders must act swiftly but sensitively. Remember, perception lies at the root of organizational climate. You can respond to deteriorating climate by changing certain conditions, yet fail to alter the climate because you have failed to account for perception. A classic mistake is to fail to distinguish between what Herzberg[58] calls "hygienes" and "motivators." Although such conditions as compensation, work conditions, work hours, and so on can seriously de-motivate employees, satisfactory redress of these so-called "hygienes" contributes little to motivation. Motivation arises, rather, out of the perceived connection between such factors as effort and reward,[59] meaningful goals,[60] and supervisory understanding and recognition.[61]

Much more could be said about the nature and significance of organizational culture and climate. My intention here is merely to introduce the concepts and sensitize you to this critical, often underestimated aspect of leadership. Perhaps I can best emphasize their importance by telling you the story of two historical leaders: Sir Ernest Shackleton and Lieutenant Charles Wilkes.

A Tale of Two Leaders

Shackleton.[62] In 1914, the specter of world war dominated the historical horizon, as it would for the next four years. Seemingly shoved out of the historical limelight with a war going on, British naval officer Sir Ernest Henry Shackleton led a crew of 28 men on one of the most ill-fated, yet remarkable exploration voyages ever chronicled. In a bid to be the first to traverse the Antarctic Continent, Shackleton set sail from Buenos Aires on October 26, 1914 on a vessel named, in what has to be one of history's most delicious ironies, *Endurance.* After a brief stop at Grytviken whaling station on South Georgia Island, the expedition set out on December 7th for Antarctica. They would not touch inhabited land again for 497 days. By January 1915, *Endurance* was stuck fast in the Antarctic ice pack. The ship would never escape the ice's grip. From May through August 1915, the crew endured four months of continuous darkness.

In September, the pressure of the ice pack caused *Endurance* literally to leap into the air and settle on its beam. On October 27th, Shackleton gave the order to abandon ship. The crew scavenged everything it could—including the three lifeboats, *James Caird, Dudley Docker,* and *Stancomb Wills*—and set out in search of open water. After three days of frantic effort, an Ocean Camp was erected on November 1st. On December 23rd (remember, this would be mid-summer in Antarctica) they again attempted to reach open water, lugging the lifeboats and all of their gear. When they managed a rate of just a mile and a half per day, Shackleton ordered the march abandoned on December 29th. After another four months of frost-bitten futility during which they killed and ate the remaining dogs and they were temporarily separated from the life boats when the ice floe they occupied split in two, Elephant Island appeared on the horizon.

On April 9, 1915, the crew of 28 piled into the three lifeboats and set out for the tiny atoll. After seven days of grueling effort, all three lifeboats landed safely on the Island and set up camp. On April 28th, Shackleton announced that he would attempt to sail the 22.5 foot *James Caird* 800 miles across the treacherous and trackless sea to South Georgia Island, the closest outpost of human habitation. This was one of the most daring and difficult navigational feats of all time, with a margin for error proportional to distant space travel. But after 17 days on impossibly stormy seas,

Shackleton and five other crew members miraculously arrived on the west coast of South Georgia Island on May 10, 1916.

They had just one additional problem. The whaling stations were on the island's eastern coast, on the other side of glacier-clad mountains thousands of feet high. After a treacherous 36-hour trek (which, by the way, was recently replicated by some of the world's greatest and best-equipped technical climbers requiring more than 48 hours), Shackleton and two companions arrived at Stromness whaling station on May 20th, 1916.

Their quest was not over. They made three unsuccessful attempts to rescue the 22 crew members stranded on Elephant Island before finally reaching them on August 30th 1916—twenty-two months after the *Endurance* had originally set out from Grytviken whaling station on South Georgia. All 28 crew members survived.

<u>Wilkes</u>. At age 40, Lieutenant Charles Wilkes was given command of the most ambitious exploring expedition ever undertaken by a Western power. Under a congressional commission to explore and chart the Southern hemisphere, discover new lands for potential American colonization and commerce, and catalog natural and cultural phenomena, Wilkes set out in late summer 1838 with six sailing vessels and 346 men on a voyage of discovery that would span four years and circumnavigate the globe. Enduring storms and shipwreck of epic proportions, the expedition rounded the Cape of Good Hope and visited places as vast and varied as Colombia, Antarctica, Tahiti, Tonga, Fiji, New Zealand, Hawaii, Puget Sound, Manila, and Singapore, to name a few.

Nathaniel Philbrick offers the following assessment of the Ex. Ex.'s (as it was known) achievements:

By any measure, the achievements of the Expedition would be extraordinary. After four years at sea, after losing two ships and 28 officers and men, the Expedition logged 87,000 miles, surveyed 280 Pacific islands, and created 180 charts—some of which were still being used as late as World War II. The Expedition also mapped 800 miles of coastline in the Pacific Northwest and 1,500 miles of the icebound Antarctic coast. Just as important would be its contribution to the rise of science in America. The thousands of specimens and artifacts amassed by the Expedition's scientists would become the foundations of the collections of the Smithsonian Institution…

Any one of these accomplishments would have been noteworthy. Taken together, they represent a national achievement on the order of the building of the Transcontinental Railroad or the Panama Canal. But if these wonders of technology and human resolve have become part of America's legendary past, the U.S. Exploring Expedition has been largely forgotten.[63]

Why is Shackleton remembered and Wilkes forgotten? Shackleton, who clearly imposed his will and exercised discipline in proportion to the extremity of his circumstances, was lionized by his men and has been canonized by history. Wilkes, whose extraordinary voyage featured leadership challenges similar in severity and, in some respects, achievements greater in significance than those of Shackleton, was loathed, ambushed, mutinied, and court-martialed. Wilkes' most ardent admirer, 22-year old naval officer William Reynolds, retracted his initial rapturous assessment of his leader and, in a secret diary of some 200,000 words, meticulously chronicled Wilkes' pathological leadership failings and flaws.

The similarities between these two leaders' circumstances and the contrasts between their exercise of *ecological* leadership could not be more striking. Both men faced adverse circumstances of incalculable proportion. Wilkes actually achieved "success." Shackleton's mission (to cross the Antarctic Continent by land) failed. Shackleton is a hero. Wilkes is a pariah. It would be a gross oversimplification to suggest that *ecological* leadership alone accounts for Shackleton's and Wilkes' vastly different leadership legacies. Whatever other leadership factors account for the differences, I nevertheless believe that their respective embrace or repudiation of *ecological* leadership played a highly significant role. Shackleton could serve as the poster child for sensing and shaping organizational climate under the most extreme conditions. Wilkes is a caricature of arrogant, insensitive, intractable obliviousness to organizational climate.

I doubt you will face conditions as extreme as Shackleton or Wilkes. I trust, however, that you will acknowledge the subtle power of culture and climate and learn to apply this primary color with increasing skill and discretion through *ecological* leadership.

Chapter Seven

Primary Color #6:
Situational Leadership

The *situational* leadership color is the most iridescent on the leader's palette. Effective leadership will cultivate the capacity to alter its hue. *Situational* leaders lead by seeking optimal fit or adaptation to variable and changing situational factors. Two corollaries issue from this reality:

- Leadership works best when there is an optimal fit between the leader and the current organizational context.
- The most effective leaders—especially in the long term— are the most adaptable leaders.

Style and Situation

You may recall my mention of the Hersey-Blanchard[64] situational leadership model back in chapter three. Figure 7.1 depicts the Hersey-Blanchard theory that different situations call for different leadership styles. A great deal of additional scholarly research and professional reflection over the past five decades has probed the relationship between leader effectiveness and various situational factors ranging and branching out in all directions, from subordinates' attitudes and maturity;[65] position-power, task structure, and leader-member relations;[66] subordinate job satisfaction and motivation, and leader acceptance;[67] management philosophy and stress variables;[68] technology, organizational philosophy, and co-worker skill;[69] and organizational life cycles,[70] just to name a few. In my judgment, no universally determinative set of style-situation factors has yet been documented. I very much doubt that such a single explanatory scheme will ever be scientifically validated. Situations and leaders are simply too complex. Ample evidence exists, nevertheless, to support the simple assertion that different situations call for differences in leaders or leadership styles.

Hersey-Blanchard Situational Leadership Model

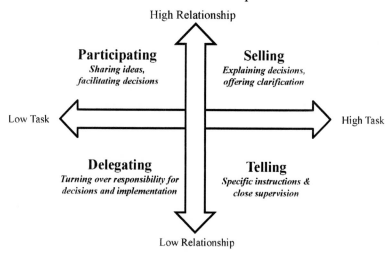

High Relationship

Participating
Sharing ideas, facilitating decisions

Selling
Explaining decisions, offering clarification

Low Task — High Task

Delegating
Turning over responsibility for decisions and implementation

Telling
Specific instructions & close supervision

Low Relationship

Figure 7.1

Psychology pioneer Abraham Maslow originated the phrase you have doubtless heard in one derivative form or another: *If all you have is a hammer, everything looks like a nail.* I know too many leaders like that. Locked within a leadership style they attribute to past successes, they become rigid and ineffective. They are puzzled when they encounter resistance, resentment and failure. Disillusionment dogs them. They know that they are effective leaders. They have experienced plenty of genuine success and earned ample, well-deserved praise. They can point to dozens, scores, even hundreds of people upon whom they have made a significant imprint. Have they lost their grip? Are they out of sync with a new generation? Are they washed up? Not likely. More likely, there is a poor fit between their well-rehearsed, trusted default style and major aspects of their current leadership context.

The implications of style-situation dynamics abound in every direction. What kind of leader is needed in a crisis? What factors most accurately predict leadership clashes? When should a successful leader give way to another in order to perpetuate success? The answer to each of these questions merits careful study and extensive reflection. I will limit my treatment in this chapter, however, to three sets of dynamics I have observed to be especially critical in terms of a leader's *situational* fit or adaptation: selection criteria and processes, organizational life cycles, and change management.

Context and Leader Selection

Many leader selection processes fail to account adequately for situational factors. Such factors are often more critical to success than specific competencies, previous experience, and surface compatibility. This is true from the perspective of both the organization and the prospective leader.

<u>Selection from Organizational Perspective</u>. Typical leadership search processes involve developing a written position description against which prospects are assessed and interviewed. More enlightened searches involve the creation of a profile in narrative or inventory form, detailing attributes of the ideal candidate for the projected role. Many organizations present to candidates information about their mission and vision statements, doctrinal creeds, governance, and overarching philosophical and policy parameters. Too few, however, engage with deep effort and transparency in reflecting upon and articulating the organization's origins, history, previous leadership, recent achievements, values, composition, context, state of financial and human resources, challenges, opportunities, and climate. In other words, many leadership search and selection processes ignore or undervalue critical *situational* factors.

A search process that adequately accounts for *situational* variables involves more than merely thinking about the role for which a leader is being sought and producing well-informed specifications regarding the character, dispositions, capacities, skills, and experiences of an ideal candidate. It also invests significant collective thought and effort into articulating the circumstances in which an organization finds itself. Different circumstances call for different leaders or, at the very least, vastly different leadership styles. Organizations court disaster when they select a leader without concerted reference to situational factors.

<u>Selection from Leader Perspective</u>. Just as organizations should consider *situational* variables when selecting leaders, leaders should devote serious thought to *situational* variables as they assess present

and future leadership roles. Leaders flirt with failure when they embark upon leadership roles without calculating the extent to which the organization's circumstances fit their style tendencies or at the very least how they will be called upon to adapt consciously their style preferences to the set of institutional variables with which they are confronted. The question is not merely whether I fit with the organization's mission and goals and whether I have the gifts and experiences necessary to fulfill the demands. I must also ask myself whether my leadership gifts and proclivities can truly fit the *situation* in which the organization currently finds itself and toward which it is projected to be moving. Incompatibilities between a leader's style and *situational* variables resemble the proverbial collision between an immovable object and irresistible force. Carnage will inevitably occur.

Organizational Life Cycles

Why is it that a leader-organization fit that appears at first to be made in heaven too often seems in the future to have been a horrible mistake? It is because organizations change. Their contours change shape. Their relationship to internal and external stakeholders evolves. Their human, financial, and facility resources and requirements undulate. Strategic realities and market conditions ebb and flow. Today's successful leader and flourishing organization can rapidly become tomorrow's flop.

As previously mentioned, decades of leadership studies have explored the relationship between a variety of situational variables and leadership styles. Wise leaders match their styles to their organization's circumstances by careful selection or conscious adaptation, or both. But organizational circumstances are not static. They are dynamic. Leaders who fail to understand this do not last long. A style that works for the leader today may well fail him tomorrow. Can anything be done? How does a leader get a handle on this?

In my opinion, Ichak Adizes[71] has produced some of the most useful insight available regarding the dynamic nature of organizations and accompanying implications for leadership selection, leadership style adaptation, and leadership team configuration. Adizes theorizes that organizations emerge, grow, develop, flourish, diminish, and die according to a consistent pattern of discernible stages, as illustrated in Figure 7.2.

Organizational Life Cycle (Adizes)

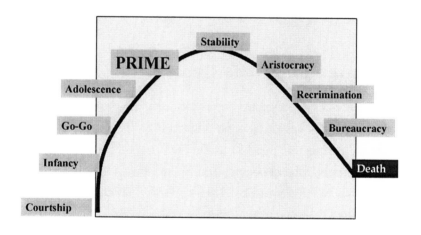

Figure 7.2

Adizes identifies and characterizes ten organizational life cycle stages as follows:

Courtship – the giddy initiation phase foaming with future focus and plenty of unrealistic dreams;

Infancy – dominated by a founder's vision and obsessed with expansion, exploitation of new opportunities, and recruiting of co-workers and partner-investors;

Go-Go – a stage of rapid growth, proliferation of activities—many of which may prove to be unfruitful—and lack of written rules or other procedural constraints;

Adolescence – in which often the founder is removed or marginalized, conflict escalates, and professional managers' efforts to impose order through policies and procedures meets with resentment;

Prime – the stage in which strategy, processes, people, and productivity are optimally aligned and the organization is at its peak of flourishing and mission accomplishment;

Stability – the subtle succeeding stage characterized by complacency and loss of direction disguised as smug contentment with the status quo;

Aristocracy – a phase in which innovative impulses are largely absent, conformity is prized, and impetus for change is suppressed;

Recrimination – an ugly stage in which scapegoating replaces accountability and the organization insulates itself from its stakeholders and strategic surroundings;

Bureaucracy – in which systems and rituals dominate but results are few and vultures are circling;

Death – no explanation necessary.

No doubt, you have already grasped the obvious. The stage Adizes labels "Prime" is the one every organization hopes to achieve and maintain. What may be less obvious is Adizes' insistence that decline in stages from "Prime" to "Stability," "Aristocracy," "Recrimination," "Bureaucracy," and "Death" is by no means inevitable. In fact, leaders who understand the cycle can recognize and even anticipate lifecycle stages and adjust the leadership mix accordingly. Therein lies the leadership challenge. More specifically, the *situational* leadership challenge involves at least four leader responsibilities.

First, leaders must lead by facilitating discernment of the organization's current life cycle stage. Ideally, those responsible for identifying leaders will have considered *situational* variables and come to consensus regarding the organization's life cycle stage and consequent leadership needs. If not, astute *situational* leaders will initiate the process, even if it costs them their jobs.

Second—reread the previous sentence: leaders must determine the extent of fit between their leadership strengths and the current life cycle stage. Not only should leaders make such a determination before accepting a leadership role, they should periodically revisit their conclusions. The dynamic nature of organizations requires leaders to recognize that success in a previous or present organizational phase in no way assures future flourishing. To assess leader-situation fit requires courage and humility. But leaders who exercise such courage can help to avoid great personal pain as well as organizational dysfunction.

Third, leaders must augment their personal strengths and styles to achieve a senior leadership configuration best suited to achieving or restoring the organization's "Prime" position. Here again, Adizes' organizational life cycle theory offers substantial additional insight concerning the interaction between leadership configuration and life cycles. Adizes posits four essential ingredients in the leadership mix of an organization: Performer, Administrator, Entrepreneur, Integrator (P,A,E,I).

Performer (P) – excels in doing what the organization exists to do, whether it be engineering, design, manufacturing, selling, shipping or, in the case of ministries, evangelizing, preaching, teaching, counseling, shepherding, justice, mercy;

Administrator (A) – organizes policies and procedures and manages resources efficiently, especially in the short term;

Entrepreneur (E) – readily senses "customer" (stakeholder/ beneficiary) needs and conceives innovative solutions and paths to long term future effectiveness;

Integrator (I) – sees the big picture and can harmonize people and processes toward optimal long term synergy.

Figure 7.3 depicts Adizes' conceptual framework regarding the correlation between various leadership configurations and various stages of the organizational life cycle. Different leadership ingredients naturally dominate in various life cycle stages. It is easy to recognize, for example, that Entrepreneurs would be ascendant in an organization's "Infancy" stage but why their continued dominance would also threaten natural progression through the "Adolescence" stage and into "Prime." On the other hand, while it is necessary for the Administrator to rise in the "Adolescence" phase in order to coax chaotic expansion into coherence and efficiency, the persistent and uncorrected transcendence of this element in the leadership mix can push the organization past "Prime" and on to the descent toward "Stability," "Aristocracy," and "Recrimination." Each element of the leadership mix is necessary at each stage, but the relationship among these leadership strengths must undergo change and correction depending upon where an organization falls upon the life cycle continuum. A "Go-Go" organization will disintegrate unless the influences of the Administrator and Integrator are elevated and released. On the other hand, the cure for a declining organization that is well past "Prime" is not better efficiency (A) but an injection of fresh ideas (I) and more energetic and unfettered execution (P).

Lifecycle Stages & Leadership Mix (Adizes)

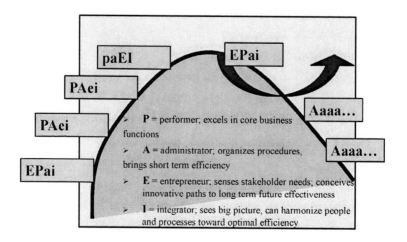

paEI   EPai

PAei

PAei

EPai

Aaaa...

Aaaa...

➤ **P** = performer; excels in core business functions

➤ **A** = administrator; organizes procedures, brings short term efficiency

➤ **E** = entrepreneur; senses stakeholder needs; conceives innovative paths to long term future effectiveness

➤ **I** = integrator; sees big picture, can harmonize people and processes toward optimal efficiency

Figure 7.3

Situational awareness and adaptability requires leaders first to identify which of the four leadership ingredients most represents their personal contribution to the leadership mix. They must then assess and build their leadership teams relative to the four primary leadership ingredients in keeping with the current *situation*. They will recognize that tension and dysfunction may signal that the organization is at a critical hinge point on the life cycle continuum and they will adjust the leadership mix accordingly. They will ask themselves whether any of the essential ingredients—Performer, Administrator, Entrepreneur, Integrator—is missing or minimally represented. Which ingredient dominates? Which ingredient(s) *should* be elevated in order for the organization to progress toward or recover "Prime"?

Fourth and, finally, leaders must gauge what adaptations of personal leadership style will best help the organization to achieve or recover "Prime." Leaders who take periodic inventory of their fit with the organization's life cycle and other situational variables need not conclude that a poor fit dictates a change in leaders. Instead, a change in leadership *style* may be indicated and entirely possible. Remember the second of our *situational* leadership propositions? The most effective leaders—especially in the long term—are the most adaptable leaders. Leadership dispositions and styles that have worked in the past may not be best in the future for that very reason. So, courageous and humble leaders ask themselves whether the changes in style demanded by current organizational circumstances fall within their leadership bandwidth. If so, they adapt themselves to new realities. If not, they have the integrity and insight to lead by initiating leadership transition and stepping aside for the sake of organizational progress.

Leading Change

Not only do internal organizational dynamics constantly change along the life cycle continuum, but also change dominates external environments in which organizations operate. *Situational* leaders understand that change is not a problem, it is a fact of life. *Situational* leadership recognizes that change is inevitable and they foster a culture of organizational adaptation. Moreover, *situational* leadership recognizes that leadership is less about *effecting* change than it is about *responding* to change. That is why I so deeply resonate with William Bridges'[72] effort to change the vocabulary of an entire sub-genre of leadership studies: change management. Bridges asserts that change is an inevitable reality, a constant. Leaders who attempt to convince their constituents to *change* are addressing the matter from the wrong angle. Instead, wise leaders work to help their constituents *respond* to change. Bridges labels the process of responding to change *transition*. If, as they say, 90% of problem solution is problem definition, Bridges has greatly contributed to the *situational* leadership challenge of change management.

Bridges offers a second insight regarding change. Leaders can help to navigate transition by recognizing that their task is not merely to persuade followers of a well-reasoned, rational case for change or to impose changes upon a reluctant constituency for its own good. Rather, they recognize that they are leading and supporting followers through an *emotional* journey. Denial is the typical response to changes in our organizational as well as our personal environments. Fear is the dominant emotion for many organizational stakeholders when they are confronted with changes they can no longer deny. Leaders who fail to recognize resistance to change as emotionally-laden and to address that resistance on emotional terms as well as on the basis of reason will inflict deep wounds upon themselves and others, undermine their efforts, and threaten the viability of their organizations.

One of the more valuable leadership insights I have been given is that emotional concerns cannot be alleviated by rational responses. This is true for all relationships. People are not looking first for the *reasons* they should not feel a certain way. They are looking for assurance that their feelings are understandable even if, in the end, you must lead by convincing them that they need to embrace a new set of realities. To one degree or another, change feels like loss to those who are experiencing it.

Leadership selection, life cycles, and change. These represent only three of the many ways in which effective leadership demands *situational* sensitivity. Your continued reflection on this aspect of leadership will doubtless lead you to recognize other implications.

To that end, perhaps it is best to end our discussion of this color on the leadership palette where we began:

- Leadership works best when there is an optimal fit between the leader and the current organizational context.
- The most effective leaders – especially in the long term – are the most adaptable leaders.

Chapter Eight

Primary Color #7:
Doxological Leadership

You might say that the seventh color on the leader's palette is the most permeable. I call this primary leadership color *doxological* leadership. *Doxological* leadership involves moving people *toward* God and moving people into step *with* God. It is the hallmark of truly biblical leadership. When a leader liberally blends this primary color with any of the others, the resulting image exudes pop and permanence. Without it, leadership devolves into self-gratification and self-aggrandizement of the leader along with exploitation and manipulation of those who follow.

You will recall that I am inclined to join the many others who prefer to define leadership more in terms of its effect than its status or activities. In the final analysis, leadership is occurring when people are following. John Maxwell has been frequently heard to quip, if you think you are leading but no one is following, you are just out for a walk. So, in the end, toward what effect does biblical leadership aim? It aims to move people *toward* God. And it aims, as Henry and Richard Blackaby put it, to "move people onto God's agenda."[73]

Leading By Moving People Toward God

Leadership is a consequential endeavor. It has the power ultimately to move people toward God or away from him, toward greater trust and obedience or toward greater autonomy. Leaders can succumb to the subtle and seductive lure of drawing people to themselves or submit to the humble and honorable call of pointing people to God. They can encourage people to trust in their own benevolence and efficacy or faithfully testify to the infinite goodness and power of their Savior and Redeemer.

To be sure, followers will be drawn to leaders. That's the way God intended it. Consider Joshua, for example. Moses' understudy takes the reins of Israelite leadership following his mentor's death. After forty years in the wilderness, God's people are once again on the threshold of promise. They've been here before. Joshua delivers a stirring speech in which he pledges himself to the Lord and exhorts Israel to join him. God's people embark by crossing the miraculously parted flood-stage Jordan River—clearly intended to evoke echoes of Moses' Red Sea parting—upon the combination mass migration and military campaign to take possession of the land. The Scripture records that, as a result, "they stood in awe of [Joshua] all the days of his life, just as they had stood in awe of Moses" (Joshua 4:14b). Few of today's leaders could claim to command the "awe" that Moses and Joshua apparently enjoyed but, as previously noted in chapter 2, both biblical testimony and professional research confirm that credibility is an essential leadership ingredient.

Here's the interesting part. This galvanization of Joshua's leadership leverage was by God's design. God both predicted it and produced it. Prior to the Jordan crossing, God disclosed to Joshua that the miracle to come was, at least in part, calculated by him to bolster Joshua's credibility. Take a look: "And the LORD said to Joshua, 'Today I will begin to exalt you in the eyes of all Israel, so they may know that I am with you as I was with Moses'" (Joshua 3:7). And so he did. In fact, I left out the first part of Joshua 4:14 earlier. Here's the full statement: "That day *the LORD exalted Joshua* in the sight of all Israel; and they stood in awe of him all the days of his life, just as they had stood in awe of Moses" (Joshua 4:14) [emphasis added]. It's pretty obvious is it not? God both predicted that Joshua would have a powerful leadership following and He produced that lifelong effect among Joshua's followers.

Why would God exalt and elevate Joshua before his people? Because Joshua was a leader God could trust to lead people toward him. Forty years before he ascended to highest office, Joshua had proven his trustworthiness on the notorious 12-man reconnaissance mission recorded in Numbers 13. The minority report Joshua and Caleb delivered didn't win the day, but God took note of it. Here was a man worthy of God's investiture. As the conquest of Canaan concluded, Joshua once again declared his allegiance to God and made it clear that would be his course regardless of whether it proved unpopular.

> Now fear the LORD and serve him with all faithfulness. Throw away the gods your ancestors worshiped beyond the Euphrates River and in Egypt, and serve the Lord. But if serving the Lord seems undesirable to you, then choose for yourselves this day whom you will serve, whether the gods your ancestors served beyond the Euphrates, or the

gods of the Amorites, in whose land you are living.
But as for me and my household, we will serve the
Lord. (Joshua 24:14-15)

Throughout his life, Joshua could be relied upon to use his God-given credibility to celebrate the One who conferred it upon him. The effect of Joshua's leadership was the consistent revelation of God's works and God's ways among God's people. If leadership is anything, it is about enhancing people's awareness of and appreciation for, as Isaac Watts[74] so eloquently puts it, "the glories of his righteousness and wonders of his love." Want to leave a leadership legacy? Make sure your leadership moves people *toward* God.

So how do you move people toward God? Surely there are many ways, but I offer three key ones for your consideration: persistence in feeding, resistance to forgetting, and insistence on fading.

Persistence in Feeding. *Doxological* leadership involves making a habit of intentionally serving as a conduit for spiritual nourishment. Remember the three primary biblical leadership metaphors we discussed in the opening chapter: *steward, servant, shepherd?* Inherent in the notion of shepherding is the idea of feeding. Feeding and leading go hand in hand. It is noteworthy that among the essential biblical qualifications for spiritual leaders is that they evidence the capacity to teach (I Timothy 3:2; Titus 1:9). Good shepherds see to it that their sheep are consistently fed and well nourished.

To be honest, I used to underestimate the importance of this leadership responsibility. I have often observed, with a degree of resentment, leaders who appeared to over-indulge in preaching and devotionalizing. Certain practices that seemed spiritually unimpeachable nevertheless felt condescending or manipulative to me, a sort of superficial, spiritual legitimizing mechanism. Spiritual rituals are no substitute for excellence in other aspects of leadership and pious posturing does not excuse leadership failures and abuses. But I have come over the years to a deeper conviction that, as a leader, God has placed people under my care, not merely under my command. So I must sincerely embrace the calling to nourish and nurture God's flock whether my leadership is exercised in a ministry or marketplace context.

How, then, can I rightly exercise the responsibility and avoid the abuses? How can I engage in spiritual feeding practices that truly lead people *toward* God? I believe there is biblical warrant to insist that a central aspect of my leadership vocation must be an intentional, lifelong pattern of helping my colleagues commemorate what God has taught us and celebrating what God has done for us. Thus, I have concluded that people are more likely to be led *toward* God when my feeding feels more like testifying and thanksgiving than moralizing and sermonizing.

Authentic teaching flows from testifying. If you aren't receiving nourishment *from* God you will have difficulty leading people *toward* God. But if you encounter God day by day through his Word and in prayer, you will find it easy to bear witness to his disclosures of himself to you. Though it was decades ago, I vividly remember an exhortation from veteran pastor, disciple-maker, and former colleague, Harold Burchett, calling for more theocentric preaching. Over the years, I have observed that Burchett was right: far too little preaching really focuses upon God. Instead, I am afraid most of what passes as talk about God focuses on sin, on our failures, on moral virtue, on spiritual duties—never really getting around to revealing or commending anything about God. I want my leadership to be theocentric. I want to lead people *toward* God. I can do so as I make it my practice simply to testify about what I'm learning about God's person, ways, and works in a way that puts the spotlight on him and not on me.

And my testifying is especially compelling when it flows from a heart of thanksgiving. I am convinced that one of the gifts of a leader is what Bill Hybels calls *holy discontent.*[75] Leaders are fueled by dissatisfaction with the status quo. They have their eyes on a better horizon. But godly discontentment can easily devolve into at least the perception, if not the reality, of ungodly ingratitude. As a leader, I must guard myself lest my desperate concern over what is not and contention for what could be should negate my deep and contagious contentment in God and celebration of what he has done.

Resistance to Forgetting. One of the greatest impediments to people's movement toward God is their tendency to forget. Every force of nature and of the spiritual realm conspires to make us forget, especially the things we most need to remember. Leaders who want to help move people *toward* God find practical ways to buttress the community's memory concerning God's covenant faithfulness along the path of their collective faith journey.

Consider Moses' exhortation to God's people at the end of a 40-year wilderness-wandering sentence imposed on an entire generation of people who may have set the world record for spiritual amnesia. Following the stupendous events leading to the Israelites' exodus from Egypt, the most advanced and powerful nation on earth, Moses is called by God to the summit of Mount Sinai where he receives the laws by which God's covenant people may flourish morally and socially and may become the marvel and envy of all nations—a beacon of true enlightenment, prosperity, liberty, and justice for all. Talk about a leadership vision!

But the Israelites get restless after waiting about a month while Moses is on the mountaintop. Concluding that this Jahweh-God appears reluctant to do their bidding and indulge their impatience, they decide to go the "designer god" route (otherwise known as idolatry). Aaron caves to their complaining and they make a golden calf "mascot god" and create their own Woodstock-like happening. Why? Gratitude is the most ephemeral of all human emotions. Within weeks, God's people *forgot* the significance of what they had so recently heard and experienced. So that generation paid a heavy price. They all died off in the wilderness, demoralized, disenfranchised, destitute, forbidden to enter the Promised Land.

Now, as a new generation stands on the threshold of all the beauty and bounty God had promised, Moses warns them: "Only be careful, and watch yourselves closely so that you do not forget the things your eyes have seen or let them fade from your heart as long as you live. Teach them to your children and to their children after them" (Deuteronomy 4:9). Three times in chapter 4 alone (verses 9, 23, 31) and at least nine times throughout the entire discourse that makes up the Book of Deuteronomy, Moses exhorts this young generation: **DO NOT FORGET!** You could easily identify this as the theme of the entire book.

Notice the suggestion in the text that forgetting is a *passive* phenomenon. Want to forget what God has taught you, what you have experienced with him? No need to do anything. Every dynamic within your heart and your world will collaborate to make you forget. What you have learned will inexorably fade from your memory. You may not wish it or intend it. But it will happen. Take it to the bank. You have God's Word on it. So, if you want to keep before you and your people the memory of what you have learned about God's nature, his commitment to you, his providential care for you, his plans for you, his vision for this world—you are going to have to be *proactive*, rather than passive.

I invite you to recognize that Scripture promotes the practice of establishing rituals and symbols that foster remembrance. The feast of Tabernacles and observance of Passover commemorated Israel's deliverance from slavery and rescue from the judgment of Egypt. Moses collected artifacts documenting God's deliverance in a chest we call the Ark of the Covenant. Joshua erected a marker from twelve Jordan River stones to commemorate the miraculous crossing into the Promised Land. Samuel erected a stone marker he called Ebenezer, a "stone of help" to commemorate God's intervention in a great Israelite victory over the Philistines. Jesus instituted Communion as a palpable, participatory ceremony in which to commemorate his atoning death, celebrate his church, experience his presence, and anticipate his return. To remember and rehearse what the Lord has done is one of the most fruitful spiritual disciplines you can exercise, personally and corporately. May I encourage you to look for means by which to help your community remember? Leading people *toward* God involves proactive measures to preserve memory and fight against the folly of forgetfulness. Leaders will move people *toward* God as they look for and latch onto opportunities to institute rituals and symbols that point one generation after another to God.

Insistence on Fading. Leaders move people *toward* God by their persistence in feeding and resistance to forgetting. They also help move people *toward* God by their insistence on fading. Perhaps that requires an explanation.

The very real, God-designed dynamic of leadership credibility is accompanied by an insidious, subversive tendency. True, leaders are enabled to lead because people are drawn to follow them.

But the responsibility of every godly leader is to resist the subtle temptations to convert their credibility into celebrity. This is a perversion of biblical leadership. As it turns out, even in the secular arena, there is generally an inverse relationship between leadership ego and leadership effectiveness. Jim Collins and his research team have documented that great companies, even great non-profits, are rarely led by people who relish the limelight. Instead, the companies that, as Collins puts it, make the leap from *Good to Great* are almost always led by individuals whose drive and determination is exceeded only by their personal humility.[76]

Even in an era when messianic speculation was at an all-time high, it is hard to exaggerate the following that John the Baptist achieved. People flocked to hear him. Though his listeners cringed at the condemnation he pronounced, they were captivated and convicted by his inescapable magnetism. Throngs followed him, hung on his every word, believed his message, and lined up to be baptized. He created buzz before we knew it was a word. And we know, of course, that this was God's doing.

What would not have been God's doing would have been for John to succumb to celebrity creep. John had a job to do. He was a witness, not the Word. He was a messenger, not the Messiah. You might say he was called to move people *toward* God. In the end, this meant he needed to seek the shadows and move off of the stage. He said so himself: "He must become greater; I must become less" (John 3:30).

Don't underestimate how hard that was. Even though John the Baptist was resolute, some of his disciples were reluctant for him to relinquish his status (see John 3:25-29). Just like John, you may well be required to rebuke and distance yourself from associates who insist upon messages and methods that diminish your affirmation that God is the only one worthy of worship and adoration and that any success you enjoy flows from his favor.

Nothing will undermine your efforts to lead people *toward* God more than indulging the inexorable pull of leadership toward personal aggrandizement. All but the most callous or naïve will reject the more blatant manifestations of the cult of celebrity. But there are plenty of less obvious pitfalls to avoid. You don't have to seek celebrity. If you are an effective leader—sometimes even an ineffective leader in a prominent office—celebrity and its trappings will seek you. And celebrity will seduce you before you know it. If you have to self-promote in order to get the opportunities you seek, you are selling out. Your capacity to move people *toward* God will be slowly supplanted by your ambition. Be vigilant—and decide beforehand that you will be the moon and not the sun.

Leading By Moving People With God

Doxological leadership involves not only moving people *toward* God but also moving people into step *with* God. Spiritual leadership recognizes that, ultimately, the force of leadership flows from God. He and he alone is the true leader to which we are leading our followers and under whose command we exercise our calling. Godly leadership is not about conjuring momentum toward self-generated goals. It is about helping people to become swept into the stream and carried along in the current of God's redemptive purposes. How can leaders help move people into step with God? By keeping their eyes on the purpose and keeping their hands off the power.

<u>Eyes On the Purpose</u>. One of the central realities of the Bible is the idea that history is headed somewhere. In fact, you really don't understand the Bible unless you realize that Scripture is not

merely a collection of religious literature or an encyclopedia of religious platitudes. Paul Tripp describes it well:

> In case you hadn't notice[d] it, your Bible isn't arranged by topic. I know that this frustrates some of you. You wish that your Bible was structured like an encyclopedia [with] alphabetized tabs on the side of the page so you could easily find your subject of interest. But your Bible isn't organized that way and that is not because of Divine editorial error, but because of Divine intention. Your Bible is a narrative; a story. Perhaps it would be more accurate to say that your Bible is a theologically annotated story; a story with God's notes. The grand, over-arching story of Scripture is meant to be the story that unpacks and makes sense of the story of your life and my life.[77]

And it is an unfolding story in which we are now participating. We have been told some things about how the story begins and how it will end. We have seen evidence of God's work throughout history to usher along the outcomes he decreed from before time began. All that we are called to be and to do should be informed by our awareness that we are playing a role in a much greater undertaking. This is true for organizations as well as for individuals.

Doxological leaders, leaders who move people into step *with* God, lead out of an understanding that their cause receives its identity, legitimacy, and meaning within the context of a much greater Cause. They consistently pray, "Thy kingdom come" with discernment and sincerity. They also recognize that "Thy kingdom come" is predicated upon on a "my kingdom go" disposition. They acknowledge that it is not enough that personal mini-kingdoms are subordinate to God's kingdom. Rather, they recognize manifestations of personal kingdoms for what they are—rival fiefdoms that stand in opposition to the One True King.

I regret to say that I have observed far too much myopia and pettiness among leaders of God's people. I had a high school teacher whose peripheral vision was progressively diminishing. He saw only what was right in front of him. I'm sure you can imagine how much mischief went on in his classes. Much of what went on escaped his notice. But he had an excuse. There is no excuse for leaders whose field of vision is severely restricted. Not only do they miss opportunities, but also they too frequently regard others' endeavors as competition or outright opposition. Jesus' disciples were guilty of this. Mark records an ugly episode in which John, speaking on behalf of all, is rebuked by Jesus after reporting that purported rivals to their ministry had been silenced (Mark 9:38-41). *Doxological* leaders exhibit a generosity and magnanimity of spirit that reflects a kingdom perspective. Their perspective extends beyond the boundaries of their efforts and embraces the farthest borders of the Divine enterprise.

Not only must our leadership activity be an expression and extension of God's grand enterprise of redemption and restoration but also it must be manifestly God-dependent. Helping followers to move into step *with* God entails helping them to realize that the impetus for their collective pursuits cannot be self-generated if it is to be God-glorifying. The fuel for our cause comes from God who is inexorably orchestrating and advancing everything toward the consummation. Prayer is the divinely-designated means by which we declare and practice our confession that God not only directs our paths but also provides the power for the pursuit. If we truly wish to lead by moving people into step *with* God, collective prayer cannot be a platitude, it must pervade our practice. I can tell you from experience that it will require every drop of your leadership resolve and resourcefulness to institute and maintain regular rhythms of corporate prayer. There will be ebb and flow. Events will conspire against you. Your adversary will oppose you. You will falter and fail. But if you want to lead by moving people into step *with* God, you cannot give up.

Hands Off the Power. No doubt about it, leaders have leverage. And the more effective the leader, the more leverage they can access. Power accrues to an effective leader. The majority becomes more and more willing to submit while the minority may be more and more easily subdued. Therein lies the potential for untold abuse. Few things can sour and skew good leadership more than a leader's tendency to coerce.

No one has been given more power than Jesus. I am not referring to his omnipotence as the second person of the Trinity. Paul tells us in Philippians that Jesus set aside his prerogative to exercise his omnipotence in order that he might take up the calling to save us through becoming a submissive, suffering servant (Philippians 2:5-8). I am referring, rather, to the authority conferred upon Jesus following his fulfillment of his redemptive calling. The resurrected Lord tells the gathered disciples on the Galilean mountain to which Jesus summoned them, "All authority in heaven and on earth has been given to me" (Matthew 28:18). All authority has been given to Jesus because he has proven that he can be trusted with it. He is unwilling to abuse or misuse it. Instead, as he has throughout his earthly life, even under the extremity of the temptations he faced in the wilderness and in the garden, he will now continue from the Father's right hand to employ the power with which he has been entrusted within the framework and according to the means of God's design.

How does Jesus use the power that he legitimately possesses, that he has so clearly earned? I cannot identify an exception to the limitation of his exercise of power in one of these two ways: (a) dispensing it to serve others; and (b) distributing it to enable others to serve. Instead of using his power to force people to submit, Jesus uses his power to serve. And rather than hoarding his power for his exclusive exercise, he lavishly delegates both authority and responsibility for others to join in carrying out God's plan. Surely this is the meaning of Matthew 28:18-20:

> Then Jesus came to them and said, "All authority in heaven and on earth has been given to me. Therefore go and make disciples of all nations, baptizing them in the name of the Father and of the Son and of the Holy Spirit, and teaching them to obey everything I have commanded you. And surely I am with you always, to the very end of the age."

Although it may seem more expedient and efficient to resort to the imposition of power to achieve desirable ends, such actions betray a willingness to rely upon personal resources rather than to recognize God's commitment and capacity to achieve what he intends. God has called you to lead in his *name*, not in his *stead*. Ramrodding is unbecoming of a servant of God. It inevitably damages people and diminishes progress. The end does not justify the means—ever. Leadership simply is not God's work if it is not done in God's way.

Doxological leaders are marked by their restraint. If God is the one leading, who are we to be forcing our will upon others? Surely we must exercise our powers of persuasion and, at times, diverge from or dismiss recalcitrant followers, but to resort to violence of any kind belies our assertion that we are moving in step with God. We validate ourselves as *doxological* leaders when we limit our exercise of power to serving and spreading it around.

What is *doxological* leadership? It is leadership that moves people *toward* God and moves them into step *with* God. That kind of leadership alone truly glorifies—or you might say—*doxoligizes* God.

Chapter Nine

Painting with a Full Palette

What is a leader? At the most basic level, a leader is someone people will follow. In other words, I prefer to think of leadership in terms of a leader's effect rather than in terms of position, intentions, or activities. Although the Bible contains many cautions about leadership and records many leadership failures, it is apparent that God calls, equips, shapes, and uses leaders as a key means to maturing and martialing his people to accomplish his purposes. He could do otherwise, but he chooses to let leaders play a part in his work.

I have attempted to demonstrate that leadership consists of at least seven major facets. This scheme represents my own attempt to make sense of the vast panoply of leadership insights available through both biblical reflection and scientific study. Others have and will come up with other very useful conceptual frameworks. Some of them are scientifically validated according to social science research methods. I make no pretense of asserting that mine is *the* biblical way of understanding leadership. I offer it only as a dynamic and potentially useful metaphor. As is the case with all metaphors, reality transcends and, in some cases, contradicts it. I nevertheless commend this metaphor for your further thought and reflection because of its conceptual breadth and its practical benefit.

By way of review, I believe leadership can be likened to an artist's palette on which are placed seven primary colors. Leaders whose palettes are supplied with all the colors and who apply their unique God-given skills and imagination will produce what can only be described as beautiful results.

Primary color #1 – *Incarnational* leadership: Fundamental to a biblical understanding of leadership is the principle that influence flows from *being* before *doing*. Leadership inescapably emanates from who you are. People follow leaders because they are credible; they walk the talk. Leaders earn credibility when they cultivate, among others, the attributes and habits of authenticity, discipline, centeredness, accessibility, growth, and grace.

Primary color #2 – *Relational* leadership: Leaders lead through authentic relationships much more than through issuing directives and implementing organizational schemes. They understand and cultivate relational health. They conduct themselves according to a biblical relational ethic. They understand their own relational style and that of their co-workers and are adept at accommodating and negotiating differences, working toward team synergy, and resolving conflict.

Primary color #3 – *Directional* leadership: Job One for a leader is to assemble a leadership team, shape them individually and collectively, and exercise leadership *through* that team. This is what the *shepherd* metaphor looks like in action. True shepherds do not engage in benign, confining, stultifying oversight. They dynamically protect, actively nourish, and fruitfully nurture those under their care. No one modeled this aspect of leadership more fully than Jesus Christ. His approach to both selection and supervision is profoundly instructive.

Primary color #4 – *Developmental* leadership: Leaders lead by helping stakeholders to clarify and coalesce around a coherent mission and compelling vision. They exercise *directional* leadership by fostering processes to ascertain mission and articulate vision and by aligning people and plans accordingly.

Primary color #5 – *Ecological* leadership: Leaders lead by exercising environmental sensitivity and skill: nurturing a community identity, engendering and espousing shared values, and cultivating a wholesome organizational climate. They understand that the success of their efforts may depend heavily upon their ability to read the signals of culture and climate and to foster conditions that permit prospering and productivity.

Primary color #6 – *Situational* leadership: *Situational* leaders lead by adapting to variable and changing situations in keeping with two controlling propositions. Leadership works best when there is an optimal fit between the leader and the current organizational context. The most effective leaders—especially in the long term—are the most adaptable leaders.

Primary color #7 – *Doxological* leadership: The hallmark of truly biblical leadership is that it moves people *toward* God and moves them into step *with* God. Leaders promote followers' movement *toward* God when they devote themselves to providing spiritual nourishment for their followers, institute symbols and rituals that guard against the tendency to forgetfulness and ingratitude, and insistently avoid seeking the limelight. Leaders help followers to move in step *with* God when they lead in seeking alignment and promoting partnerships toward God's broader purposes and when they lead their communities to rely on God's power through prayer.

Americans have generated a variety of quips to describe persons who appear not to be making full use of their intellectual faculties. Among the insults I have heard are the following: *His pilot light has gone out. She's a few French fries short of a Happy Meal. Her elevator doesn't go all the way to the top. He is about half a bubble off on a three foot level.* I could go on. Readers from other cultural and linguistic backgrounds can supply similar sayings.

One of our more familiar slams alleges, *He's not playing with a full deck.* I'm afraid that when it comes to leadership, too many of us are not painting with a full palette. Leadership is a gift, but it is a gift that comes with some assembly required. It is both an art and a science. Or, as is true in the case of all art, both talent and technique are required in order to produce a work of significance.

It is my hope and prayer that many aspiring and experienced leaders will benefit from the reflection this book may stimulate concerning the vast and beautiful possibilities inherent in God's vivid leadership spectrum. Not all leaders have the same capacity. God's gift of leadership comes in uneven measures of quantity and variety (Romans 12:8). But the degree of leadership accomplishment is not exclusively proportional to the gift. The grace of godly leadership also depends on the degree to which the gift is developed through input, exercise, and reflection. Leaders have little chance of reaching their potential if they fail to commit themselves to learning about and honing their capacities to exercise leadership in all its facets. How much of your palette is still neglected?

End Notes

Introduction

1 Larson, E. (2003). Devil in the White City: Murder, Magic and Madness at the Fair That Changed America. New York: Crown Publishers.

2 Maxwell, J. C. (Rev. Ed., 2007). *The 21 Irrefutable Laws of Leadership: Follow Them and People Will Follow You*. Nashville: Thomas Nelson, p. 16.

3 Engstrom, T. (1976). *The Making of a Christian Leader*. Grand Rapids: Zondervan.

Chapter 1 – Leadership in Biblical Terms

4 Sanders, J.O. (Rev. Ed., 1980). *Spiritual Leadership*. Chicago: Moody Press.

5 My first encounter with the exposition of these concepts was in Hian, C.W. (1987). *The Making of a Leader: A Guidebook for Present and Future Leaders*. Downer's Grove, IL: InterVarsity Press.

6 Howell, D.O., Jr. (2003). *Servants of the Servant: A Biblical Theology of Leadership*. Eugene, OR: Wipf & Stock Publishers.

Chapter 2 – Primary Color #1: *Incarnational Leadership*

7   Kouzes, J.M., and Posner, B.Z. (4th Ed., 2008). *The Leadership Challenge.* San Francisco: Jossey-Bass, A Wiley & Sons Imprint.

8   Kouzes, J.M, and Posner, B.Z. (2003). *Credibility: How Leaders Gain and Lose It, Why People Demand It.* San Francisco: Jossey-Bass, A Wiley & Sons Imprint.

9   Ibid, p. xiv.

10 McDonald, G. (December 20, 2009). *The Secret Driven Life.* Christianity Today Online (http://www.christianitytoday.com/le/currenttrendscolumns/leadershipweekly/thesecretdrivenlife.html).

11 Coe, J.H., and Hall, T.W. (2009). *Psychology in the Spirit: Contours of a Transformational Psychology.* Downers Grove, IL: InterVarsity Press, p. 228.

12 Elmore. T. (2004). *Habitudes: Images that Form Leadership Habits and Attitudes.* Atlanta, GA: Growing Leaders, Inc.

13 Loehr, J., and Schwartz, T. *The Power of Full Engagement: Managing Energy, Not Time, Is the Key to High Performance and Personal Renewal.* New York: Free Press (Simon & Schuster).

14 Johnson, P. (2009). *Churchill.* New York: Viking-Penguin, pp. 109, 114.

15 McNeal, R. *Practicing Greatness: 7 Disciplines of Extraordinary Spiritual Leaders.* San Francisco: Jossey-Bass, pp. 83-84.

16 Lencioni, P. *The Five Temptations of a CEO: A Leadership Fable.* San Francisco: Jossey-Bass.

Chapter 3 – Primary Color #2: *Relational Leadership*

17 George, B. (2007). *True North: Discover Your Authentic Leadership.* San Francisco: Jossey-Bass, pp. 28-29.

18 For an excellent exposition on the theological/psychological pathology of this syndrome, see Coe, J.H., and Hall, T.W. (2009). *Psychology in the Spirit: Contours of a Transformational Psychology.* Downers Grove, IL: InterVarsity Press (chapter 14, especially pp. 288-289).

19 Goleman, D. (1995). *Emotional Intelligence.* New York: Bantam Books.

20 If you're ready to seriously assess your emotional health, try self-administering the *Inventory of Spiritual/Emotional Maturity,* found in Scazzaro, P. and Bird, W. (2002). *The Emotionally Healthy Church.* Grand Rapids: Zondervan. Also accessible at www.emotionallyhealthychurch.com.

21 McNeal, R. *Practicing Greatness: 7 Disciplines of Extraordinary Spiritual Leaders.* San Francisco: Jossey-Bass, pp. 10ff.

22 Robinson, B. (2009). *Incarnate Leadership: Five Leadership Lessons from the Life of Jesus.* Grand Rapids: Zondervan, pp. 23-25.

23 Covey, S. (Rev. Ed., 2004). *The Seven Habits of Highly Effective People: Powerful Lessons in Personal Change.* New York: Free Press (Simon & Schuster).

24 McNeal, R. *Practicing Greatness: 7 Disciplines of Extraordinary Spiritual Leaders.* San Francisco: Jossey-Bass, pp. 61-80.

25 Clinton, J.R. (2009). *Finishing Well: Factors, Enhancements and Barriers.* J. Robert Clinton Institute. http://jrclintoninstitute.com/resource-store/articles/finishing-well-factors-enhancements-and-barriers/

26 See Clinton, J.R. (2009). *Reading on the Run: Continuum Reading Concepts.* J. Robert Clinton Institute. http://jrclintoninstitute.com/resource-store/articles/finishing-well-factors-enhancements-and-barriers/

27 Collins, J. *Good to Great: Why Some Companies Make the Leap … And Others Don't.* New York: Harper Business.

28 Kouzes, J.M., and Posner, B.Z. (4ᵗʰ Ed., 2008). *The Leadership Challenge*. San Francisco: Jossey-Bass, A Wiley & Sons Imprint, pp. 20-21.

29 Hersey, P., and Blanchard, K. H. (1982, 4ᵗʰ Ed.). *Management of Organizational Behavior: Utilizing Human Resources*. Newark: NJ: Prentice-Hall.

30 Schluter, M., and Lee, D.J. (2009). *The Relational Manager: Transform Your Workplace and Your Life*. UK: Lion.

31 Blake, R., and Mouton, J. (1964). *The Managerial Grid: The Key to Leadership Excellence*. Houston: Gulf Publishing Company.

32 Pearson, J. (2008). *Mastering the Management Buckets: 20 Critical Competencies for Leading Your Business or Non-Profit*. Ventura, CA: Regal.

33 Bolman, L.D., and Deal, T.E. (3ʳᵈ. Ed., 2006). *Reframing Organizations: Artistry, Choice, and Leadership*. San Francisco: Jossey-Bass.

34 Lencioni, P. (2002). The Five Dysfunctions of a Team: A Leadership Fable. San Francisco: Jossey-Bass.

Chapter 4 – Primary Color #3: *Developmental Leadership*

35 Bruce, A.B. (1886). *The Training of the Twelve*. New York: Harper.

36 Engstrom, T. [Timothy J. Beals, Ed.] (2007). *The Essential Engstrom: Proven Principles of Leadership*. Colorado Springs, CO: Authentic Books.

37 Sweet, Leonard – cited at the following URL: http://jmm.aaa. net.au/articles/15883.htm

38 Kouzes, J.M., and Posner, B.Z. (4ᵗʰ Ed., 2008). *The Leadership Challenge*. San Francisco: Jossey-Bass, A Wiley & Sons Imprint.

39 Finzel, H. (1994). *The Top Ten Mistakes Leaders Make*. Wheaton, IL: Victor Books, pp. 97ff.

Chapter 5 – Primary Color #4: *Directional Leadership*

40 Levitt, T. (1960, May-June). "Marketing Myopia." *Harvard Business Review*, #38, p. 45.

41 Nesbitt, J. (1982). *Megatrends: Ten New Directions Transforming Our Lives*. New York: Grand Central Publishing.

42 Hybels, B. (2008). *Axiom: Powerful Leadership Proverbs*. Grand Rapids: Zondervan, pp. 17-18.

43 Kouzes, J.M, and Posner, B.Z. (2003). *Credibility: How Leaders Gain and Lose It, Why People Demand It*. San Francisco: Jossey-Bass, A Wiley & Sons Imprint, p. 241.

44 Hybels, B. (2008). *Axiom: Powerful Leadership Proverbs*. Grand Rapids: Zondervan, p. 52.

45 Bell, Anthony, (May 2010). "Leaders as Story Makers." *The Leadership QuickBrief*. Online newsletter: www.leaderdevelopmentinc.com.

46 Collins, J. (2000, June). "Aligning Action and Values." *The Forum*. (http://www.jimcollins.com/article_topics/articles/aligning-action.html).

47 Collins, J. (2001). *Good to Great: Why Some Companies Make the Leap ... and Others Don't*. New York: Harper Business.

48 DePree, M. (2004). *Leadership is an Art*. New York: Broadway Business.

49 Groeschel, C. (2008). *it: How church leaders can get it and keep it*. Grand Rapids: Zondervan, p. 60.

Chapter 6 – Primary Color #5: *Ecological Leadership*

50 Plueddemann, J.E. (2009). *Leading Across Cultures: Effective Ministry and Mission in the Global Church*. Downers Grove, IL: IVP Academic.

51 Ibid., p. 71.

52 Collins, J.C., and Porris, J.I. (1994). *Built to Last: Successful Habits of Visionary Companies.* New York: Harper Business, p. 220.

53 Pearson, J.W. (2008). *Mastering the Management Buckets: 20 Critical Competencies for Leading Your Business or Non-Profit.* Ventura, CA: Regal Books, p. 124.

54 Hybels, B. (2008). *Axiom: Powerful Leadership Proverbs.* Grand Rapids: Zondervan, pp. 112ff.

55 Babbes, G.S., and Zigarelli, M. (2006). *The Minister's MBA.* Nashville, TN: BH Publishing, pp. 30-31.

56 Best Christian Workplaces Institute. (http://www.bcwinstitute. com/)

57 Anderson, N., and West, M.A. (1996). "The Team Climate Inventory: Development of the TCI and its Implications in Teambuilding for Innovativeness," *European Journal of Work and Organizational Psychology, Vol. 5, Issue 1, pp. 53-66.*

58 Herzberg, F. (1966). *Work and the Nature of Man.* New York: Thomas Y. Crowell.

59 Vroom, V.H. (1964). *Work and Motivation.* New York: John Wiley.

60 Locke, E.A. (1968). "Toward a Theory of Task Motivation and Incentives." *Organizational Behavior and Human Performance,* vol. 3, pp.,157-159.

61 Heider, F. (1958). *The Psychology of Interpersonal Relations.* New York: John Wiley.

62 Lansing, A. (2001). *Endurance: Shackleton's Incredible Voyage.* London: Weidenfeld and Nicolson.

63 Philbrick, N. (2003). *Sea of Glory: America's Voyage of Discovery: The US Exploring Expedition.* New York: Viking-Penguin.

Chapter 7 – Primary Color #6: *Situational Leadership*

64 Hersey, P., and Blanchard, K. H. (1982, 4th Ed.). *Management of Organizational Behavior: Utilizing Human Resources*. Newark: NJ: Prentice-Hall.

65 Halpin, A.W. (1966). *Leader Behavior of School Superintendents*. Columbus: College of Education, Ohio State University.

66 Fiedler, F.E. (1967). *A Theory of Leadership Effectiveness*. New York: McGraw-Hill.

67 House, R.J. (1971). "A path-goal theory of leader effectiveness," *Administrative Science Quarterly*, Vol. 16, pp. 331-339.

68 Blake, R.R., and Mouton, J.S. (1964). *The Managerial Grid*. Houston: Gulf Publishing Co.

69 Reddin, W.J. (1970). *Managerial Effectiveness*. New York: McGraw-Hill.

70 Adizes, I. (1990). *Corporate Lifecycles: How and Why Corporations Grow and Die and What to Do About It*. The Adizes Institute (www.adizes.com; ISBN-10: 031744267).

71 Ibid.

72 Bridges, W., and Bridges, S. (2009, 3rd Ed.). *Managing Transitions: Making the Most of Change*. Boston: Perseus, De Capo Lifelong Books.

Chapter 8 – Primary Color #7: *Doxological Leadership*

73 Blackaby, H. and Blackaby, R. (2001). *Spiritual Leadership: Moving People Onto God's Agenda*. Nashville: Broadman & Holman.

74 Excerpted from "Joy to the World," based on Psalm 98, from Isaac Watts' 1719 collection, *The Psalms of David: Imitated in the language of the New Testament and applied to the Christian state and worship*.

75 Hybels, B. (2007). *Holy Discontent: Fueling the Fire That Ignites Personal Vision.* Grand Rapids: Zondervan.

76 Collins, J. *Good to Great: Why Some Companies Make the Leap ... And Others Don't.* New York: Harper Business.

77 Tripp, P. (2009, May 27). *Psalm 73: The Old Story.* [Blog post.] Retrieved from http://paultrippministries.blogspot.com/2009/05/psalm-73-old-story.html.

CPSIA information can be obtained at www.ICGtesting.com
Printed in the USA
LVOW122341220213

321204LV00001B/2/P